BELIEVE IT OR NOT

This book is a follow-up to the book,
"You Won't Believe This."

"A compilation of true, short stories."

Published by
YVM Books
3426 Crow Mountain Rd
Russellville, AR 72802
USA

Printed in May 2017 by YVM Books

Copyright ©2001 by Yan Venter
All rights reserved/ No part of this book may be used or reproduced in any manner whatsoever without written permission except in the case of brief quotations embodied in critical articles for reviews.

For information:

YVM Books
3426 Crow Mountain Rd,
Russellville, AR 72802, USA.
WWW.yanventer.com
Email: ekke4god@gmail.com

TABLE OF CONTENTS

INTRODUCTION 6
THE UGLY TRUTH 7
IN A HOLE 14
SNAKE IN THE SACK 17
A STRANGE THING AMONGST FLOWERS........................25
CUT THE GIANT'S HEAD OFF 29
THE LOVELY SUZIE 40
AN ANGEL NEXT TO MY BED 45
GOING TO THE COURT OF HEAVEN 49
GREG DOTSON AND THE BEER BOTTLE 55
"DEMON POSESSED" LIONS 61
THE 'INDIANA JONES' FIASCO. 79
A DREAM ON FIRE 90
ANOTHER AIRPLANE SAGA 100

INTRODUCTION

For many years, many people have requested a book of this nature.

The intention of this book is not to present me in any particular way, but only to offer the highest praise to the Lord, God Almighty.

At the same time, I hope as you read through these amazing stories, that you will be inspired to settle with the thought that God is at work in our lives at all times.

There's absolutely nothing the enemy can bring against us that God does not already have covered.

The reader must understand that the Lord is never caught unawares and therefore has to come up with certain emergency measures to keep our boat afloat. No, He has our lives planned out long before it happened.

Finally, may this book also serve to inspire you to seek and do the will of the Father.

THE UGLY TRUTH

I was pastoring my first church in Fort Victoria, Rhodesia,[1] in the early seventies. It was a fairly big, small town and the people were known as being friendly and hardworking citizens.

Rhodesia had become the target of Communism which at that time, was the main threat. The country was by enlarge a Christian country

The leader of the country, Mr. Ian Douglas Smith, was a politician, farmer, and fighter pilot who served as Prime Minister of Rhodesia (or Southern Rhodesia) from 1964 to 1979. The country's first premier not born abroad, he led the predominantly white government that unilaterally declared independence from the United Kingdom in 1965, following prolonged dispute over the terms. He remained Prime Minister for almost all of the 14 years of international isolation that followed, and oversaw Rhodesia's security forces during most of the Bush War, which pitted the unrecognized administration against communist-backed black nationalist guerrilla groups.

These so-called guerilla fighters were mean terrorists who stopped at nothing to intimidate the local people.

When I arrived in Rhodesia in the early '70's, the country was at the height of the war and every available man was involved in that fiery battle in one way or another.

---

[1] Now known as Zimbabwe. (Situated in the Southern Region of Africa.)

At first, I was serving as youth pastor to that church, but within the next year, the pastor left for America and I was asked to become the pastor.

The first few months went by as usual and the church grew rapidly. However, the dark clouds of war and the ugly face of terrorism was looming as a clear and present danger over everyone.

At exactly nine-o-clock on a Monday morning, the doorbell rang. My mother, who was visiting with us at the time, answered the door.

After a while, she came into my room and said, "Yan, there's a military officer asking for you." I frowned and asked her the question as if she should know, "What does he want from me?"

She smiled and said, "I guess that's for you to go and find out!"

I walked into the sitting room and the young sergeant was standing, waiting on me, and when I walked into the room, he introduced himself and pulled an envelope out from under his left arm.

He handed the envelope to me, saying, "Pastor, you've been drafted into the war to serve in the special forces should you pass the training."

For a moment I was stunned. I did not know if I should be happy or concerned. Several years before, I volunteered to the South African Forces, but they turned me down because of my flat feet.

I found myself in a position for which I did not know that I was prepared for now that I was a pastor of a church. I expressed it to the Sergeant, "Sir, I you sure? I am a pastor of a church."

The Sergeant smiled and spoke to me as he walked to the door, "I guess you will have to state your case to the commander when you keep your appointment this Wednesday morning. Your appointment is at ten." With that, he excused himself and left me standing in the middle of the room.

Bessie walked into the room and asked what the man wanted. When I told her what just transpired, she said, "But, you're not even a citizen of the country, Yan? How can this be?"

"Well honey, I guess I will find that out on Wednesday. For now, we'll just have to wait to worry," I said smilingly.

On Wednesday, I was directed to the commander's office in a typical government office.

The dark brown furnishings comprised of a small desk with two hard, straight-back chairs opposite him and a tall filing cabinet. The floor was old concrete that have seen better days. Mr. Ian Smith's picture was the only decoration on the wall and a dirty ceiling fan was circling lazily, obviously losing the battle against the murderous heat.

The Commander was in his late forties and his uniform was neatly pressed. He proudly displayed a thick mustache and when I walked into his office, he politely got up from behind his desk and shook my hand. In front of him was my file and he formally crossed his two hands, leaning his elbows on the desk.

A fly was crawling around the brim of his hat and when he moved his head, the darn thing did not even move.

"I understand, you have questions to ask me, Pastor?"

Suddenly, I did not feel like any objection was going to work, but I mentioned it to him since he obviously was informed by the visiting Sergeant to our home.

"Sir, yes sir. I did mention to the sergeant that I was a pastor of a church, and did not know how I was going handle killing people some days and trying to save them on Sunday's?"

A kind smile came to his face when he spoke. There was no arrogance about him, but only the stern affirming of his position as Commander.

He smiled and then carefully explained to me that I would be in the pulpit most Sunday's. "Pastor, you've been drafted into one of the most elite fighting forces. You will serve as an anti-terrorist fighter and only be called upon to act, following a terrorist strike when it happened, should you pass the vigorous training."

I felt excited about the prospect, but had to ask the next question. "Colonel, I am not reluctant to serve. In fact, I'm excited about it, but the thing I'm wrestling with is this; how will I be able to kill during the week and then preach again on Sunday's to get people saved?"

He smiled and then replied in a friendly, yet stern manner. "Pastor, I am also a child of God, and in fact, most of our soldiers are, and they all deal with the same question. This is not a war we asked for. We are not fighting 'people.' We are fighting evil. Communism is a dark force which makes it their task to come against Christianity."

He paused for a moment while I remained quiet. The fly made his move into the man's face and he took a wild swat at the filthy insect. He grabbed a plastic fly swat and for a moment it seemed as if he had forgotten I was still there. He was now concentrating on getting the forbidden insect. As soon as the fly sat down on the file in front of him, his hand came down and with a loud noise, the fly came to its sudden death.

"These bloody flies are such a pest, pastor. I guess, they're like the terrorists we fight. They are just not good for anything.

I sat in silence and knew that him and I at least had that much in common. I hated these flies as much

As if he completed a major task, he turned his attention back to me and made a suggestion.

"Pastor, I'll tell you what we'll do. Let's first take you through the training. If you pass that, then let's send you on your first mission so that you can see for yourself what we're all dealing with. If you still feel so strong about this matter, then we'll give you an office position. We need help there also."

I could not help but to like the man. He was very considerate, and I knew I would enjoy to serve under him.

"Colonel, thank you, sir."

The training was indeed rigorous and when it was over, I was excited to learn that me and my little group of soldiers were commissioned to go and investigate a horrible terrorist attack against a little mission church "in the sticks," as were described by the Rhodesians. "The sticks", meant "In the bush", or deep into the country away from ordinary civilization.

We functioned in small groups of five men. Our task was to start where the hostilities took place and then to track these offenders down and to bring them to task. It did not matter where they fled to, we would make it our business to make them pay.

I was still not sure how I would feel about all of this. My mind was working in all different directions, but when we arrived at the little church, there was no sign of any life. Over in the distance, a lonely donkey was grazing on thin grass. The rest of the yard was just red sand. It was very hot as usual and as we walked around the little church to get to the front door, we came to a shocking halt. One of my men brought a handkerchief to his face.

The two, white missionary ladies, were pinned upside down to the door posts of the church. They were badly mutilated and hanging upside down with flies crawling all over them. It was a sight I would never forget!

One of our men heard a sound and as we investigated, we found a little black lady, hiding behind some bushes. At first sight, I thought she had something hanging from her face, then at closer look, I noticed it was flies that was crawling all over her. She was very weak from blood loss and near death. The terrorists left her so severely scarred. Because she did not want to betray Christ, they cut her entire bottom lip off and part of her lower chin.

At that moment I knew beyond a shadow of doubt, I could fight in this war. I could and would handle a rifle to make that evil pay for their deeds, and when I eventually returned to face the Colonel, I told him that in no uncertain terms.

I fought side by side by some of the bravest souls I ever met and my life was certainly enriched by the many experiences in the bush.

IN A HOLE

The Government set a curfew that started at 10:00 pm and lasted until 5:00 am every day. During that time, no one was allowed to move around. One of our tasks in the war was to "sweep" through areas with suspicious activities during the curfew hours.

One particular night, the five of us were doing a sweep in a treacherous area where pioneers of old, left many holes in search of gold and diamonds. Many of these holes were very deep and after time collected dangerous debris. Should one fall into one of them, the chances of serious injury or even death were almost hundred percent.

That activity was done under cover of darkness so that we could remain unnoticed by the enemy.

That particular night was cloudy, and therefore the danger was exponentially higher. We were walking in a straight horizontal line, separated three to five hundred feet from each other depending on the terrain.

Suddenly, we heard one of our comrades cry out in distress. He fell into one of those holes but managed to grab hold of a root of a tree. The weight of his backpack did not do much to help his grip, and he shouted all the louder for help.

"Hold on, Hansie," we are coming, I cried out, but because of the danger of stepping in one of those deathtraps ourselves, we could not move fast.

Hansie was an experienced soldier and a man with a strong character. He was the kind of person which any of the platoon leaders would want to have in their group.

He was not only a great soldier, but Hansie was also a good friend to all of us.

His agonizing cries prompted us to move faster than we were supposed to, putting our lives at risk also.

"I cannot hold on much longer," Hansie was crying out.

This soldier was tough. He was a farmer and used to milk his cows, twice a day. I knew he had strong hands, but his grip could not fold around the large root because of the way it was coming out of the ground.

We could not see his position and therefore had to move toward the sound of his voice.

"Keep on talking, Hansie," one of the men cried out. "We cannot see you."

From the sound of his voice, I could tell I was getting close to him, but then heard this faithful friend cry out; "Guys, I'm slipping. I'm not going to make it; please take care of my family. Jesus, I thank you for your grace in my life."

I launched forward when I reached the hole where the drama was taking place. I yelled at the top of my voice, "Hold, Hansie! Hold!" I threw myself forward in an attempt to get a hold of his hand, but I was just too late.

The unfortunate man fought the pull of gravity until he could not anymore, and then ...

He dropped only six inches!

Hansie had no way of knowing that the pit he fell into, was as shallow as it was. After pulling him out of the pit, we sat down with him in sweet relief and laughed about the moment.

There's a lesson to learn from that experience.

Often we are holding on to situations which we fear may bring calamities into our lives. The Lord wants you to let go and trust him for the rest. Sure, you may not know how far you will drop, but be assured, the Lord will not allow you to go through something He does not know you can handle.

Learn to trust and obey, for often there's no other way…

SNAKE IN THE SACK

During my service as a member of the Rhodesian Special Forces, I experienced many adventures, which served to enrich my life.

Some of the stories were either serious or sad, while others were more on the funny side.

On one such occasion, after moving through the bush for days, we approached a village far away from any civilization. For several days, as we moved deeper and deeper into the native Shona land, we came upon a group of three young black boys, about ten or eleven years of age.

They were fishing by a stream and had no idea of our approach until we were right behind them. We announced our presence with a soft grunt. Those boys turned, and when they saw us standing behind them, they threw their primitive fishing gear into the air, screaming at the top of their voices, and without taking another look at us, ran with all their might to the nearest village where they lived.

All the way as they ran, we could hear their screaming, so we decided to head in that direction to announce our presence and to find an explanation for their fear.

As we approached the entrance to the village, several elders were waiting for our appearance, and when we finally did, the chief elder greeted us in the usual Shona Custom.

As soon as he was comfortable with our introduction, he sat down on a nearby log which had been placed there for that purpose. The other men followed suit and positioned themselves in a half circle.

One in our group spoke fluent Shona and explained our presence to the kind leaders of the village.

The women and children were keeping their distance but remained near enough to follow the discussions.

The familiar scene with chickens meandering around the village and goats grazing on nearby leaves was typical.

I wondered to myself if anyone knew which was theirs or if anyone cared? It was clear that capitalism was the farthest thought from anyone's mind.

We made "soft talk" for a while before we come to the real issue. I wanted to know why these boys and many others were so afraid of us.

The chief smiled at me as the soldier interpreted my question. He did not hesitate even one little bit and replied as follows: "The reason these boys are scared of you is that you are the ugliest thing they have ever seen.

He threw his head backward and laughed out loud with the other men joining him. While he laughed, I shuddered as I looked into the poor soul's mouth. He had almost no teeth. Many of them broken off by the gum and I was wondering how he could handle all the pain.

We joined them in their laugh, although we knew we were laughing at ourselves. For a while, I was thinking, how dumb it was.

Suddenly, he stopped laughing, and when he did, it seemed like a sign for the others to stop laughing also.

The man was visibly carrying some level of authority in the camp because when he barked out instructions to the nearby women, they immediately turned and hurried into the village with the kids following.

Henry, the Shona affluent member in our group, explained to us what just happened. "He instructed them to prepare dinner for us, and boy's, we had better accept the offer." He explained it was the Shona way of showing respect and honor to a guest.

The sun was already setting low on the horizon, and because we did not allow ourselves the privilege of opening up canned food earlier for lunch, we were more than happy to accept the invitation.

We were more than ready to get a warm meal, and although we realized there was no telling what to could expect on the menu, we silently decided to leave it as a pleasant surprise.

None of us realized how hungry we were, till the aroma of the upcoming meal, filled our nostrils.

During the conversations that followed, my eyes scanned the area for suspicious activity, but nothing of interest caught my attention.

Finally, one of the Pikaneens came and whispered in the ear of the chief elder that food was ready.

The friendly old man stood up, and when he did, the rest of his men followed suit.

My young friend, Jim, stood next to me and whispered, "This is going to be interesting, Yan."

I smiled and answered, "if you don't like what you see, close your eyes and enjoy the meal. Imagine it to be something else."

Jim smiled and responded, "That's the one thing my Mother told me I don't have."

"And what is that?" I asked back softly in our language.

Jim smiled and replied, "Imagination, son. I don't have any imagination." When I looked over at him, he was not smiling.

We were invited to sit down at what seemed like the dining area. In the middle was a cozy fire with the thick coals of hardwood reminding us of the one common fact between all people. Fire!

Very humbly, two of the local "mamma's" moved to the large pot on the fire. Curiously I leaned forward to see what was in it but Henry punched me in the side, and when I looked at him, he motioned to me to cut it out. I smiled at him and reluctantly decided to control my curiosity.

One of the worst times in my life is at Christmas when some of the gifts around the tree have my name on it. I would do my level best to get people to make a slip, and I'd get a chance to know what was in the box.

My mind returned to the present when one of the Mamma's appeared before me with a fairly big bowl, neatly carved from wood. The dish consisted of a stew of Mopani worms, cooked in milk.

I smiled and thanked the friendly lady in front of me, while I keenly observed the young Jim next to me. He had turned a solid white in the face and nervously glanced over at me, but when he found no response, his glance went further toward the smiling Henry who was already digging into the meal. He pulled a fat, long worm from his bowl with his fingers, placing it on his lip and sucking it down like spaghetti.

Jim turned even more white in the face as I followed the example of Henry. I was surprised to find the meal tasty, and before long, I helped Jim to finish his also.

After taking our leave from those friendly humans, we moved about an hour north to bed down for the night.

Although the territory sported all sorts of wildlife, the biggest threat to our sanity was snakes, spiders, and scorpions, all of whose bite could be fatal.

We have all learned about the hair-raising stories from fellow soldiers, and their experiences with those unwelcome visitors in sleeping bags.

As we approached our camp for the night, silence was of the utmost importance.

Should anything compromise our position, we would have to break up camp to move elsewhere. As we bedded down, each finding a cozy spot within arm's range, soft whispers of "good night", were exchanged and it did not take any of us long to drift away.

The days were hot, but the nights were amazingly brisk.

As usual, Jim bedded down to my one side, while Thomas, bedded down to my other side.

Thomas was a strong, athletic type of person. He was a typical "civilized outdoors person." The kind who enjoyed the outdoors as long as there was enough comfort. He never murmured nor complained under any conditions, but he always found a way to make things as comfortable as possible.

With the zippers pulled safely up to the chin, a pull string around the neck closed all and any openings into the sleeping bag to keep unwelcome guests away.

I've been with that small group of anti-terrorist fighters for almost two years. We've all grown fond of each other and learned how to rely on each other's strengths.

Thomas was a quiet but friendly, Rhodesian. A fourth generation farmer who lived and farmed the same place as long as he could remember. I've never been in contact with a perfectionist till I met Thomas. I am also a kind of a "neat-freak", but nothing like this him.

For Thomas, everything has to be in their correct place. I have often observed his mannerisms before bedding down. Each night everything had to be done in the same order.

It took him forever to prepare a soft mattress, made out of soft grass.

The evening was unrealistically quiet and peaceful. Even the general chorus presentation of toads and crickets seemed to be absent. I waited in vain for the familiar jackal call, but then I slipped away into sleep oblivion.

The peaceful silence and quiet rest suddenly gave way to a long and miserable shout, and it came from Thomas!

The four of us were up, out of our sleeping bags, each holding onto our rifles, ready to make war when we noticed Thomas had not moved. Although he was the one crying out in misery, he did not move.

"There's a snake in my bag," he yelled out again. The place where we found ourselves, were known for many kinds of venomous critters. It was therefore not uncommon for one of those critters to try and find warmth. Several soldiers have reported snake bites at moments such as that one.

"Lay still Thomas, lay dead still," Henry instructed him.

"Yan, you grab the zipper on the other side, and at the count of "three," we unzip his bag. Hansie, you deal with the snake", as Henry handed him a forked stick. We all had our head lamps on and shone down at Thomas' shaking person.

For that moment, nobody was thinking "terrorists." The world had finally turned back to "normal" as we readied ourselves to deal with a situation in nature.

That place was known to have all sorts of snakes, some of which were deadly.

After what seemed like an eternity, I finally responded to the sound of "three."

Thomas was laying there, paralyzed by the moment. Hansie was standing in a menacing posture over Thomas. The moment was serious. Each one of us had our friend's safety in mind.

As we pulled the zippers down, simultaneously, we grabbed the top of the sleeping bag and pulled it open. Thomas was laying there like a mummy in only his underpants and a small T-Shirt. His underpants had Mickey Mouse printed front and center.

None of us noticed the underpants at first because we were scanning for Mr. Viper.

"Where is it, Thomas?" Hansie asked, still standing ready to spear the foe.

With a tone filled with fear, Thomas replied, It's right there next to my right leg, guys. Come on man! It must be in clear sight."

Hansie leaned forward and moved the snake next to Thomas' leg. When Hansie did so, Thomas shrieked in agony as Hansie, and the rest of us broke out in laughter.

The snake turned out to be Thomas's arm.

During the night, he laid uncomfortably on his right arm, causing it to go numb. Automatically, the cold arm found its way into the sleeping bag. When it touched the rest of his body, he thought it was a snake.

With a sheepish grin on his face, he finally offered to make coffee.

The commotion compromised our position, and we moved on early.

A STRANGE THING AMONGST FLOWERS

Several days had gone by with little sign of any human activity. My unit dragged themselves to each next point in the unbearable heat of the day.

For as many days we were fighting the monotony of each dull day. We were trained to be on the lookout for feelings such as we were experiencing. We would change formation or add a different points man. Whatever worked to add a new environmental awareness, we did.

The little that we saw in human activity always brought new life to the group, and we tried to learn as much as we could from each encounter.

For several weeks, we have had little encounters with humans, but the one thing that stood out above all others were the fact that there was no sign of modern civilization.

We turned out to be the highlights of their lives in many cases, as they have never seen a white skin, nor a nose the size of Thomas'.

He certainly sported a display of a "Royal Nose," underlined by a thick, bushy mustache.

That particular day turned out to be different, as we broke into a clearing and there in front of us, was the strangest phenomenon.

A relatively new model Toyota motor car. What made the sight different though, was that the car had four flat tires, but surrounded by the most beautiful flower garden. It was obvious that much care was given to keep the garden up.

Peeping through the window of the car made the riddle even greater. The car was relatively new, but looking through the window, one could tell that the front seats displayed wear.

Suddenly, we heard a stern voice behind us, and we all turned around, startled by the man.

"What are you doing in my house? Who the h...l are you and what interest do you have on my car?

All of us took a step back from the vehicle, and our interpreter expressed to him our most profound apology.

The reader has to understand the setting of a typical African "home."

When you notice a typical village of huts, you must know that each establishment of shelters in a circle, belongs to one family. Each housing generally accommodates a wife with her children. Many times, one man can have as many wives as he can afford.

Normally, each settlement has an opening where a large tree or structure of sorts indicates the entrance, or as we would refer to it, "the front door."

Many an uninformed European or a visitor from another part of civilization, found themselves in deep trouble when they would "enter" the front door without knocking and waiting for permission or an invitation to come "inside."

Walking through the opening and entering the "Kraal" would be as insensitive as when anyone merely walks into your home without an invitation.

We had just fallen prey to such a stupid or ignorant trespass, and it took a lot of skilled talks to get the chief to forgive us.

Finally, we were invited to sit at the opening with the head and several other prominent men in the group.

Our conversation was cleverly designed not to go directly to the subject of the car. We had to first talk about other more important matters, like his children, wives, and ancestors, before we finally were allowed an opening to speak of the car and the now familiar flower garden.

From what we could make out, was that one of the chief's son's made a move to further his education in the big city.

It appeared from what he was trying to explain to us that his son entered his father's name into a completion of sorts, and his dad won the car!

The brand new car was driven many miles into the thick bush territory and delivered to the chief.

He was so impressed with that beautiful, shining object that he gave instruction to his Pikkaneens to build him a garden around it so that it would look even more impressive.[2]

He entertained each distinguished visitor who came to see him inside the beautiful smelling vehicle. Using the car, no one could convince him of it. To him, it was merely an ornament and nothing else.

Slowly, the wheels lost its air, and the battery ran down flat.

---

[2] This really DID happen.

The key was still hanging in the ignition, the engine was still inside under the hood of the car with less than three thousand miles on the odometer, but it remained useless, as there was no way to start the vehicle anymore.

We were all stunned at what we saw. It was an unbelievable sight, to say the least.

Later the following morning, during my quiet time, God spoke to me, saying, "Yan, that is the state of so many of my people. I've given them the most incredible vehicles to use in my Kingdom. Vehicles like prayer or many of the most unusual gifts and so on, but they merely keep them on display, and never turn the key to feel the vehicle come alive.

Dear friend, as you read this story, why not ask God, which one of those vehicles remain stationary in your life, but not used at all.

Ask the Holy Spirit to air up what has become flat in your life and to give you an electrical "jump" to get the powerful engine started which will allow you the ability to reach many more "Places" in your life.

Walking with God is a continuous, miraculous and supernatural adventure.

CUT THE GIANT'S HEAD OFF

It was in the early seventies. I had just accepted the pastorate in Fort Victoria, Rhodesia, as senior pastor.

With the help of God, the church was growing rapidly.

Although I completed Bible school and passed all the subjects with excellent grades, I realized how little I knew about people once I started pastoring.

Therefore, I made it my responsibility to move as close as possible to the senior men in the church, learning from them as fast as I could. The rich knowledge base nestled between the gray hairs of many of those parishioners often served me well in the work of the Lord, as I opened those "treasure chests" and discovered many gold nuggets inside.

Although I am now a seasoned servant of the Lord, I still value those treasure deposits in the lives of so many men and women.

During the first months of my first church in Rhodesia, a lovely young lady, Barbara, came to our church as a guest of one of our young couples.

Barbara was in the late teenage years of her life. I learned that she was the daughter of one of the richest men in the territory. A man who showed no respect to the church. Someone who openly confessed himself to be an Atheist.

She was listening attentively to the sermon, and when I gave the altar call, she was one of the first ones to respond.

I noticed a nervous twitch in her face when I stood in front of her to pray. When I talked to her, explaining the easy steps to accept Christ as her Savior, she suddenly fell at my feet, totally manifesting a state of demonic possession.

Two of my strongest deacons were commissioned to carry her to my office.

The moment I stepped into my room, I recognized that it was going to be a long fight to get a victory.

Looking back today, I will never do things the same way again, but I was young and inexperienced. I was not able to recognize those demons were toying with me and the deacons, and the cute "darling'" was enjoying the attention.

We prayed and wrestled with those demons until the wee hours of the morning. Those demons often spoke to us through Barbara with a thick, male tone of voice.

Finally, Barbara would "Wake up"[3] from the apparent trance she found herself in for those hours and went home, herself exhausted.

That night as I fell down on the bed next to Bessie, entirely spent, Bessie, wanted to know what had happened and if she was set free.

To my utter dismay and shame, I had to confess defeat.

---

[3] In later years, the Holy Ghost taught me different. Each demoniac had control over their actions; no matter how many demons were inside. Cf The maniac of Gadara with a thousand demons inside him.

"Wow, honey," Bessie enquired from me; As a servant of God, why don't you have the authority to cast those demons out of her?"

My answer did not carry much weight when I said, "Baby, I'm too tired to try and answer your questions now.

At the breakfast table the next morning, Bessie was sitting at her place to my right, and as soon as I said "grace", she was ready with her question again.

This time, I had no excuse to her intelligent questions. She let me have it in a loving way.

"Baby, maybe you need to pray and fast more," she suggested in a friendly but accusing way.

I merely smiled as I finished my breakfast, but excused myself as soon as possible to get to the office. Much work was waiting on me there, and to me, it was going to be a way of escape.

The following Sunday, Barbara was back, and the same pattern followed the altar call. The same two deacons carried the "victim" to my office and once again, the prayer and spiritual wrestling carried on till the early hours of the morning when she would decide she had enough.

This pattern continued for several weeks until I dreaded each coming Sunday.

Although the people loved me and no one said anything, the questions that Bessie confronted me with, was obviously in the minds of my flock also.

I was humbled and felt defeated. During the weeks in-between those Sundays, I studied every possible occurrence of possession.

During some of those exorcism attempts, demons would do all sorts of strange things to impress us as we allowed it.

One evening, while she was lying flat on her back, the demons asked for a pen and paper and we complied with their request.[4]

While Barbara was holding the pen with only two fingers at the back of the pen to the journal, the demons controlled the pen and in seven different handwritings, wrote to me in the seven languages I could speak. Each message said, "I hate you, and I am going to destroy you!"

After Barbara had gone home that morning, I remained in my office, praying and seeking the face of God.

"Lord, this cannot continue like this. I need an answer, my God."

I remembered the instruction of Jesus who told the disciples that many of these demons don't come out but by prayer and fasting.[5]

---

[4] It is something I would never comply with today. Demons love attention and when you allow them freedom to talk and play, they will "entertain" you for hours. Those days I learned one thing, at the command of the Name of Jesus, they MUST leave, otherwise the "victim" enjoys their presence.

[5] Mark 9:29; Matt 17:21

I went home, telling Bessie of my decision. "It will end this week. I've had enough of this. It cannot continue one week longer."

Bessie smiled as she walked up to me, putting her arms lovingly around my waist, saying: "That's the man I know. I was waiting for you to say that, baby. Now we're going to see the Holy Ghost work through you."

For several days, I separated myself and dedicated my time to prayer and fasting. On the third day, the answer came to me.

The Holy Ghost asked me the question, "How did David slay the giant?"

Without even thinking long, I replied, "with a stone, my Lord!"

I thought the question was pretty easy and straight forward but was intrigued when the Lord did not agree with my natural response.

"But Lord, what does this have to do with the casting out of demons?"

There was a short period of silence, and then it was as if the Lord said, "I'm waiting for your answer…?"

"Lord, I honestly thought David slew the giant with a sling?"

Suddenly I remembered the correct answer and joyfully proclaimed, "With his sword," I said. He killed the giant with his sword. He chopped his head off right there."

I started to laugh at myself. The answer to that question was there all the time, but like many other things in the Bible, we read over the answers as we already have tradition controlling our thinking.

When I shared my experience with Bessie upon my arrival, she also asked the same question, "but honey, what does it have to do with Barbara and the demons?"

I remember shrugging my shoulders and said, "We'll have to wait and see, baby. Just wait and see."

That coming Sunday, I was sitting on the platform when Barbara walked in again. Silence and a thick atmosphere filled the place as she entered. By now, people did not feel good about the incident.

My mind went back to a few days ago when the Lord reminded me about David and Goliath, and how Goliath died. As she walked into the church, I smiled by myself, because I still did not know how the answer to that question related to the situation with Barbara. All I knew was that the Lord was about to give me the victory that night.

When Barbara "collapsed" on the floor again during the altar call, without any emotion in my voice, I instructed the two usual deacons, "carry her to the back. I will deal with her after the service ended."

This time they carried her like a sack of beans and laid her down on the floor in my office, and while one of the deacons and his wife remained on guard, the other one left. He was glad to be excused after the many weeks of struggle. My instruction to the other deacon and his wife were to do nothing until I arrived.

34

During all the other experiences, we could not get Barbara to communicate with us. She was seemingly unable to hear us.

The moment I walked into my office, suddenly I knew what to do.

I stepped over her prostrate body who were once again, dressed provocatively. I reached for the telephone on my desk and called her father. The very wealthy atheist who did not believe in spirit beings.

"Mr. Burger," I said as he picked up the phone. "This is Pastor Yan Venter, of the Church of God, in town. He grunted acknowledgment, but I continued as if his approval did not matter.

"Sir, your daughter is laying on the floor of our church, totally demon possessed. She apparently enjoyed the attention, but I have no more patience to play her games. Please come and collect your daughter."

Before he could answer anything, I abruptly hung up the telephone. When I did, the little spoiled Princess on the floor suddenly opened her eyes, sat up straight, and asked, "Why did you do that for?"

The atmosphere suddenly changed, and for the first time, I was in charge when I said, "Oh, the little wonder CAN hear us?

She wanted to grab her purse to leave, but I grabbed it first and said, "While we wait for your dad to arrive, Barbara, let me tell you how dangerous the game is that you have been playing here, week after week."

She remained cornered in the office as I took the time to explain to her how easy God can set her free. "Barbara, they are not your friend, and unless you are willing to release them, your life will turn into a living hell.

Her dad arrived and loudly announced his presence outside by sounding his horn loudly.

She left the building and followed him home in her car.

Bessie felt alarmed, wanting to know what I was going to do about the situation.

"I'm now going to the Giant's home to settle this once and for all."

Bessie let me know without any hesitation; she would not go with me.

I smiled as I started my little pickup truck and headed outside town, where they lived high up on top of the only hill in that territory.

As I entered their gate, I was impressed with the steep driveway, properly lit with tall light poles. All sorts of squirting fountains put up a gorgeous display of perfection.

When I got out of my car, I noticed a long flight of stairs leading up to the mansion.

Mr. Burger himself, leaned over the wall on his porch, looking down at me, and then arrogantly barked an instruction out to me.

"Get the h…l out of my place!"

I looked up and said, "Mr. Burger, I'm not here to bother you, but I believe you must take the time to listen to me. It is to the benefit of your daughter."

His wife appeared next to him, and she ignored his instruction when she said, "Pastor, please ignore my husband. Please come up sir; I need to know what is going on."

Mr. Burger was an angry man, and the action of his wife did not help matters much at all. He uttered full instruction to his well-trained Doberman Pincher dogs to ATTACK.

The two dogs came running down the steps toward me. I stood my ground and waited for the dogs. When they came close to me, I pointed my finger at them and loudly exclaimed, "YIELD, IN JESUS NAME!"

To the astonishment of the angry man upstairs, the two dogs came to a halt, lowered themselves to the ground and merely growled.

I walked up the stairs to their house and left the two dogs behind me.

Mr. Burger did not wait for me but turned away cussing, and I never did see him again.

Mrs. Burger apologized for the behavior. She was obviously different from her husband and invited me to sit down.

"Pastor, thank you for coming to our house. Please explain to me what has been happening with my daughter."

I took the time to explain every bit of detail to her. Before I left the church, I placed the demonic notes in my pocket. I then presented them to Mrs. Burger, asking if Barbara spoke any of those languages.

"No Sir, the only language she speaks is English," she replied. For the following minutes, I took the time to explain the entire debacle to her.

Finally, the devoted mother thanked me and asked if I would do everything in my power to help her daughter.

When I left their property, I said to myself, "well, that will be the last I see of Barbara."

I knew the Giant had been knocked down and that night, the Lord helped me to cut his head off.

The following Sunday evening I almost fell off my chair when I noticed the arrival of Barbara once again.

I did not know if I should be happy or upset.

Throughout the sermon, Barbara cried with her head lowered into her hands. When I gave the altar call, she responded as before, but that night things turned out different. When she fell down on the floor, manifesting demons again, I stepped down from the platform and commanded those demons only once to come out of her.

With loud screams, one demon after another left her and finally she started crying out the name of Jesus, asking Him to save her.

That evening, Barbara Burger was indeed set free and became a devoted child of the King.

Not too long after that experience, we left Rhodesia and never saw her again…

THE LOVELY SUZIE

I had often said, "when God made the man, but He outdid Himself when He made the woman."

In fact, I'm of the opinion that few women are not pretty in one way or another, but then there are those who are exceptional in their looks.

Friends of Bessie and I are living in the beautiful town, called Sabie, in the eastern part of South Africa.

It is located 360 kilometers[6] east of Johannesburg and is 64 kilometers[7] west of the famous Kruger National Park. It is known for its scenery and beautiful waterfalls and is a popular tourist attraction.

Its primary industry is forestry. The plantations surrounding Sabie comprises of one of the world's largest human-made forests.

Suzie and her husband have been living in that beautiful town, nestled in a deep valley on the escarpment of the Drakensberg mountain range in the Mpumalanga ("place of the rising sun") province of South Africa.

She was one of the more strikingly beautiful women I knew. She had beautiful, long hair and her eyes, decorated with the most beautiful eyelashes which she knew how to use to attract attention when she needed to.

---

[6] 224 miles

[7] 40 Miles

She also displayed teeth so white and perfect. I have often said, "they have the appearance of pearls."

Together with those, she also had other assets which attracted even more attention.

I recall sitting in my car one day as she came walking in my direction. A stranger, walking in the opposite direction, passed her by, and when he did, turned his head to stare at her from behind as she rhythmically worked her perfectly shaped hips.

The unfortunate individual kept on walking as he stared, and walked into a telephone pole next to me. I could not help but laugh at him, and the humiliated individual cussed at me when I did.

Yes, Suzie was strikingly beautiful!

Once I told my wife, I thought Suzie had discovered the secret to youth, because as many years went by, she remained the same, and still caused men to walk into telephone poles, or fall over their own feet.

Early one morning as I was passing through Sabie with a bus full of youth, we suffered a breakdown and needed help.

The sun was just about ready to stick its head up above the eastern horizon, when I walked onto the porch of Suzie and her husband's house, seeking help for my problem.

The doorbell loudly announced my presence at their front door.

Their two poodle dogs, loudly protested as they pressed their front paws against the bottom of the door, barking. A light came on in the sitting room, while a man's voice rebuked the two menaces from the inside.

Waiting for the door to open, I thought it must be my friend dealing with the nervous animals.

A woman answered the door without turning on the porch light. As the door opened, the light from the inside washed over me, but not enough for her to make out my features.

"Good morning Ma'am," I said as the older lady opened the door.

Because of the poor light, I was not able to make out the person, and for just a moment I thought it was possibly the mother or a visitor to my friends.

She reached for the switch and turned on the porch light. I took a moment to speak because the older lady seemed familiar. Before I could speak, the woman in front of me did, by exclaiming, "Yan!?"

Suddenly it dawned on me who the lady was. It was Suzy!

A Suzy whom I've never seen before.

She did not have long hair, she had short, gray hair.

She did not have pearly, white teeth. In fact, she did not have a tooth in her mouth!

She did not have long eyelashes; she hardly had any at all!

I stuttered through my embarrassment as I exclaimed loudly, "My goodness, Suzie. I did not recognize you in this poor light."

Her husband came into the sitting room and helped me get through the uneasy moment.

While Suzie made me coffee and her husband excusing himself for a moment to get dressed to go and help me, I sat there with this bewildered thought.

"TODAY, I HAVE SEEN SUZIE FOR THE FIRST TIME!"

All the other times, I may have seen "MAX FACTOR," or some other beauty aid. I smiled at my thoughts.

Much later that morning, when we were on our way again on the bus, I spoke to the Lord, making fun about my embarrassment.

I said, "Lord, did you see Suzie this morning?"

I giggled by myself and for a moment could not help but laugh at my memory of the real Suzie openly.

Then the Lord spoke to me, and a lesson came out of the experience, when the Lord said, "Yan, that's the way it is with many of my children. They regularly wear

43

masks when they come to me, not realizing I see them at any time of day or night.

Their masks of pretense or masks of hypocrisy keep them from entering my presence."

The lesson went on for some time longer as the Lord encouraged me to remember to appear before Him with an honest face, and not the popular, spiritual "Max Factor" which the church wears so often.

The hypocrisy in the Church has been a significant blame for the unnatural look of the Christian.

I know that none of us like to expose the real me to everyone and in a certain way, all of us carry masks as we move around other humans. That's pretty reasonable, but when we approach the Lord, let us come as we are. Remove the cover because God, like David, states it in Psalms 51:6 says, "Behold, Thou desirest truth in my inward parts; in the hidden part Thou shalt make me know wisdom."

AN ANGEL NEXT TO MY BED

"Honey, you need to slow down," Bessie said to me after I received a phone call from our organization's head office. I was invited to attend a business meeting in Pretoria, about four hours' drive away from where we lived.

Although Bessie has always been one hundred percent behind me in the ministry, her calm but a very intelligent way of looking at things, served me well through the many years of our marriage but also in the ministry.

As the years passed by though, I learned to pay closer attention to her opinions or advice. At that time, however, we were married for no more than ten years, but the problem was, I operated mostly at "top speed."

The Congregation outgrew their facilities at that point, and we were involved in the completion of a large, beautiful, new facility. The building projects heavily taxed my person. The Stewardship Campaign which stretched over months of intense involvement added significantly to my stress levels.

To save money, we were owner builders. Although I was blessed with able men to handle a project of that size, they were all very involved in their jobs and so, that responsibility rested on my shoulders.

Toward the second half of the project, we also started with the construction of our first home. That was once again happening against the advice which Bessie offered.

She suggested to get the church construction out of the way first, then take a break before starting the house.

I was unwilling to delay the building of the house, because the construction team I used at church, was willing to build the house at a reduced price, providing I allow them to flow into the house construction without a break in-between.

As a young, athletic man, always energized by significant challenges, I could not understand why Bessie and anyone else for that matter, wanted to "sabotage" my plans with the idea of rest!

"Rest is for the night," I always smiled and said, stubbornly each time Bessie would mention that idea. "The construction workers are the ones working and in need of rest," I debated her suggestion.

In fact, the idea of slowing down did not fit well in my thinking. I was healthy, I was energized, and according to my thinking, my level best happened when I was pressed from different sides.

The "slow down" idea from Bessie before leaving home that morning to drive to Pretoria did not sit well with me. It caused a "boil-over" in my spirit, and I left the house upset. With the radio playing soft, Christian music in the background, I allowed my mind to weigh everything Bessie was saying.

"She is correct," I said to myself, as I considered the weight, resting on my shoulders. The two construction jobs, my involvement in numerous committee's in our town as well as in our Organization. I was considering the many demands of the growing church and the time it took from me to get it all done.

The thing which Bessie said was suffering the most, was my time with the family.

"Yan," she said, "what shall it profit a man, if he shall gain the whole world, but lose his family...?"

I smiled while I was thinking about the intelligent way she used the scripture to emphasize her argument, but I conceded to her point.

About twenty minutes out of town, I had just made up my mind to step away from some of the many unimportant things and to offer more of myself to my family when suddenly things went wrong in my head.

Things started spinning fast, and it felt as if the blood rushed to my face. In fact, it felt as if I was held upside down while the blood rushed out of the bottom of my body to my head.

Suddenly I started feeling cold and shaky. Knowing something was amiss, I turned back to where I come from, but when entering town on my way home, I could not put any facts together. It was like everything had a loose end. I knew I was a pastor, but could not tell you of which church. Nothing seemed familiar, and I found myself driving up and down, one street after another. It was as if I suffered amnesia. A man working in his garden waved a greeting when he saw me, so I stopped my car and walked across the street to him. I could tell he recognized me, but my head was spinning faster and faster.

I never reached him but collapsed in the middle of the street. They rushed me to the hospital, and for the next seven days, I remained in a coma, totally unaware of my surroundings.

On the seventh day, I came out of the coma, but as I became aware of my surroundings, I noticed the room was full of family and friends. Bessie was standing next to me, crying. My mother was on the opposite side, and she was crying. Around the bed were pastor friends of mine with my two children, CJ and Reynette, standing with their heads hanging.

I had wires and tubes in different parts of my body. It felt as if I was literally "wired" to a machine. I had two sets of I.V.'s and wires connected to my heart. An oxygen mask over my face made me feel sick.

The ones who weren't crying were praying. I had no idea what was going on, but the severity of my surroundings was more than I could handle and I went back into a state of unconsciousness for another seven days.

When I finally came out of that state of unconsciousness, the room was empty except for a lady dressed in white, sitting on a chair next to me.

Although I did not feel sick, I remember feeling feeble. I had my head turned toward the lady who was talking to me as if we have been in the conversation for a while. In fact, she spoke to me in a familiar way. While she spoke, I was trying to place her. She looked familiar in a strange way, and although my head was not spinning anymore, I just could not put her in my mind.

Before I could say anything, she continued where she was with the "news" she was delivering to me. She said, "and you know, Yan, we have called and called, but no one has shown up?" She sighed and looked at me.

I was apparently staring at her with a confused look, when I asked, "Who have you called, and who was supposed to come and who are you?"

She smiled but answered only half of my questions.

"Pastors, Yan. Pastors! I need someone to pray for the dying man in the cubicle next to you, but they have not responded to my calls."

I did not answer her but kept on staring at the woman sitting next to me, with confusion apparently written all over my face, when she continued by snapping her fingers as if a sudden revelation came to her.

"Say, YOU'RE a pastor, aren't you? Without waiting for a response, she continued; "Do you think I can get a wheelchair to push you next to his bed so that you could pray for him?"

I could not believe my eyes or ears. I was in an Intensive Care Unit of the hospital, and she wants me to pray for another sick person! I was stunned, to say the least.

Finally, I got the words out and said, "Ma'am, I'M SICK!"

That little lady in white, responded apologetically, saying, "I'm sorry, Yan. I should not have asked that of you."

I must have blinked because the next moment she was gone. She disappeared.

I realized it must have been an angel who paid me a visit.

The rest of this story is explained in my other book, "You Won't Believe This."

Friend, as you read this, remember what the Bible says in Hebrews 13:2, "Be not forgetful to entertain strangers: for thereby some have entertained angels unawares."

GOING TO THE COURT OF HEAVEN

When you pray to God, you are bringing your Complaint against the devil, or Petition for your financial need or healing or other desires before the divine Heavenly Courts before the Righteous Judge. It is, therefore, imperative that you learn divine courtroom procedures and presentation of testimony and submit and allow Jesus to testify on your behalf.

Your "prayer" may be a declaration of rights and liabilities and enforcement of those rights. For the return of something stolen or for an injunction to stop the demonic harassment of the enemy. Also for the reconciliation of relationships, for monetary damages, for a better job, for success in business, for good grades in school, for a spouse, for a healing of body or soul, or for mercy and justice while you are here living in the world system.

There is nothing you cannot bring before the Heavenly Courts. In the Heavenly Courts there is a distinction made between the law courts and the equity courts, so you must know the difference in the type of requests for which you put in your prayer at the end of your Complaint or Petition.[8]

Several years ago, Reynette, our daughter, have just divorced her husband and father of her daughter. The man was not good news for her. He was a drug addict and been in prison several times in his young life. He was lazy and unwilling to work. When he still succeeded in finding employment, he was unable to keep it for long.

---

[8] This is an excerpt from an article by: Dr. Nova Dean Pack, "Prayer Puts You in God's Heavenly Courts"

The entire situation was a nightmare for her and also for us. The only way she could make ends meet, was for us to step up financially.

Reynette knew she made a terrible mistake, but for the longest time, she tried to make a success of her marriage. We knew things were bad but were unaware of the fact that the man beat up our daughter, until one day we showed up at the house and found her beaten and severely bruised. He used a cue stick on her.

She finally decided to accept our advice and successfully filed for a divorce. Not long after the divorce, the man was once again arrested for housebreaking and theft, and he ended up with a ten years' imprisonment sentence.

Although the court granted her sole custody of the child, she felt it right for his parents to see the child, but another nightmare started. That grandmother had an agenda of her own, and reported the slightest scratch on the child to Child protection services and dragged Reynette into one situation after another.

On one occasion, they sent the police (who were friends of them) to our home to forcefully come and remove the child to them. My wife's sister was visiting with us at the time from South Africa, and her daughter was the same age as our granddaughter. The cops seized the wrong child, and the entire debacle played off in the street with neighbors watching it.

Following that horrible experience, Reynette decided to move to Ohio to start a new life.

Several months after we all relocated to Ohio, Reynette received a subpoena to appear in court, back in the state of

Texas. Because she did not have the funds for an attorney, the court appointed one for her.

We were all hoping that he would be a worthy representative for her, but the day of her appearance, I traveled back with her to Texas, and the moment we met the attorney, it was clear that he was a no-good, worthless individual with zero interest in her case.

She had tried on several occasions to talk to him on the phone to before the court case to establish a relationship and to find out about his plans to represent her, but could never make contact with him, and neither did he ever call her back.

Five minutes before the court started, the sloppily dressed attorney showed up. When he introduced himself to us, it was evident he had no interest in us, and neither had any time for us to ask questions.

I realized Reynette was facing a dangerous situation, so I excused myself and stepped outside. It was time to call on my advocate, Jesus, our Intercessor, and Mediator. I took a few minutes in prayer to lay out our case and asked the Lord to step in for us in the matter.

In the court, the grandparents showed up with a high paid attorney. He was well-prepared and well-spoken, and when he got up to speak, he demanded attention.

The man told all sorts of lies about us to the court and not one time did Reynette's attorney say anything or objected to any of the lies, even though Reynette tried in vain to point the lies out to him.

The lying attorney told the Judge that we are South Africans with the intention of taking the child out of the country. He asked the court to grant guardianship to his clients.

Once again, Reynette's attorney sat there with his head hanging forward and not opening his mouth even one time.

When it was finally his turn to speak, the Judge asked him if he had anything to say, and to my amazement, the man did not even make an effort to stand up. "No, your Honor, I have nothing to add," he said.

Reynette's jaw dropped with astonishment. Even the Judge seemed surprised as he looked at the poor excuse of an attorney.

I lifted my eyes to the Lord and said, "Master, I need your help, please.

Then the unspeakable happened! The Judge looked over at me where I was sitting in the pews behind Reynette.

In a friendly manner, he asked me, "And who are you, sir?"

I rose to my feet and greeted him respectfully. "Your honor, I am the other grandfather, Reynette's dad.

To the amazement of the highly polished attorney on the other side, the Judge asked me in plain talk, "Grandpa, what do you have to say about this matter?"

For the next few minutes, the Judge allowed me to speak freely, and it enabled us to present our side, giving me a chance to point out the lies of that attorney. Then he asked me again, "Grandpa, how would you resolve this matter?"

Heaven moved to interrupt the affairs on earth at that moment.

My words were spoken calmly and filled with genuine compassion. I said, "Your Honor, to be quite honest; I don't think this matter even belongs in court. It is only correct that the grandchild must know both grandparents on either side and we have no objection at all. Although the mother has sole custody, we have no problem allowing those grandparents the right to see the child as often as is practical. We stand ready to receive instruction from the court to bring the child to Texas. All we ask is for them to pay expenses one way and we the other. Your honor, all they have to do is to talk to us when they want to see the child."

Their attorney jumped up to add more nonsense, and the Judge silenced him. "I have heard enough from your side, and I am ready to rule on this matter."

The other grandmother raised her hand to speak also, and the Judge acknowledged her.

With a nagging tone, she added, "Judge, I am a Christian, and I have prayed for two weeks about this court case," but the Judge silenced her. He said, "Ma'am, I'm so glad you prayed, because God answered your prayers, and He sent me that Grandpa over there."

Silence fell over the court. Never before in my life have I experienced the tangible presence of the Lord, more than that moment.

The Judge instructed me to fetch the child to visit the grandparents for two weeks and for them to pay the expenses one way. He told their attorney to mediate the matter with me.

"Grandpa," he said and smiled. "If you have any problems, you come directly to me," and he adjourned the court.

The other grandparents disappeared without even talking to us, leaving their attorney to make arrangements with us.

Reynette and I went back to Ohio and returned the following day with the child. Upon our arrival, their attorney apologetically informed us that the grandparents do not wish to see the child!

I insisted we pay a visit to the Judge who agreed to see us immediately. After listening to the clumsy explanation of their attorney, the Judge looked up at me with a smile and said, "Grandpa, it certainly seems as if someone is looking out for you and your daughter. This matter would have been a lifelong issue for her, coming and going over long distances. I now release your daughter from any further responsibilities. This issue is now closed and you will NEVER have to appear before me with this case again."

To the reader, this is a lesson you can learn. We don't have to go into the battlefield against an unseen enemy. We have an invitation from Heaven itself, to approach His throne boldly to present our case. God is the Heavenly Judge, who will rule in a righteous way.

GREG DOTSON AND THE BEER BOTTLE

"Now concerning spiritual [gifts], brethren, I would not have you ignorant." (1 Cor. 12:1)

These are the words of St. Paul to the church at Corinth. However, please note the word, "gifts," are italicized in that verse. That means, it is an added word.

Italicized words were first used in 1560 when an edition of the Bible, known as the Geneva Bible, appeared. This Bible had been prepared by the Protestant reformers in Geneva and was translated directly from the original Hebrew and Greek. In it, some words had to be added in English to make the meaning plain, although they were not necessary for the original idioms. Languages cannot be translated word for word. The translators, then, distinguished such necessarily added words by italicizing them. The Geneva Bible became the most popular Bible of its time.

By the beginning of the seventeenth century, there were three versions of the Bible in England, but these translations were by no means correct, and as time went on, the meaning of some of the English words changed. The need for a better translation became apparent, and from this need came the most used version even today, the King James or Authorized Version. King James, The First, gave the task of translation to a group of 54 translators, and in their translation, they followed the lead of the Geneva Bible translators and made use of italics for added words.

In most cases, italicized words clarify the meaning of certain phrases. However, because these translators were not necessarily inspired by God in their work (though some would claim so), they made mistakes.[9]

Now, therefore, if we read our text verse without the "added" word, it will read as follows: "Now concerning spiritual brethren, I would not have you ignorant."

My opinion on this verse is that the added word was not needed. By allowing the addition, it changes the focus to the gifts instead of the person. I believe, Paul was saying, that the spiritual people, are to be noted. God assists them by arming them with incredible abilities. To some, he adds this, and to others, He can add that, and so on.

The reason for the little exposition in this book of short stories is because I want the reader to understand what Paul meant when speaking about spiritual men and women of God.

He was saying, "People who walk with God are endued with incredible powers or abilities. Don't underestimate them.

Through the many years of walking with God, I have often found myself astounded by many of His servants.

Don't make the mistake of merely evaluating them from what you see on the "outside."

My friend, Greg Dotson, is one such individual. Not only is he a great businessman and in love with the Lord, but a

---

[9] This quote is taken from THE CHURCH OF THE GREAT GOD. www.cgg.org

great servant in the Church where he serves in whatever capacity his pastor may ask him to help.

I have always known him to be a humble servant, but as I moved closer to this very tall, successful business man, I became more and more impressed with the way he allowed God to use him.

Bessie and I were in the process of building an orphanage in Kenya, Africa.

For many years, we have been sending funds to a local pastor couple, who were in charge of our work there.

Because of our love for the children in Kenya, and a strong desire to build a proper building for an orphanage, we channeled many resources to that area.

For several years we have been sending funds through to the local pastor. Not only did we build them a nice three-bedroom home, but we also purchased the necessary property for the upcoming Orphanage.

A young, Architect friend of ours in Dallas, TX, designed a beautiful building for us, free of charge. I invited Greg to accompany me to Kenya so we could evaluate the situation for the upcoming construction.

The moment we arrived in Kenya, this great friend of mine, looked at me and said, "Brother Yan, I don't know what it is, but there is something wrong with this pastor."

It was something I did not want to hear. The pastor was an older man but appeared to be humble. At first, I brushed Greg's observance aside, but he kept on insisting.

A few more times, he repeated himself to me, until I decided to invite the pastor to a prayer meeting at our hotel.

Sitting around a table in the small central office or lobby of the hotel, we bowed our heads for prayer, and I remember asking the Lord to give us direction.

The pastor next to me was sitting with his head bowed, but not praying at all.

Greg was pacing the small room, and I was trying to allow my spirit to make contact with God.

The room was in bad need of dusting and flies have been allowed to make the place their dwelling. No one seemed to have any problem with their invasion. The high temperature and the smell of dirt and dust filled the air.

For several minutes we have been waiting on the Spirit of the Lord. I had my mind set on the visitation of the Lord when suddenly I heard someone placing something on the table in front of my face.

I opened my eyes and stared straight into an empty beer bottle which Greg placed loudly in front of me.

While staring at the bottle, I wondered why he would do something like that?

I looked over my right shoulder to Greg, and instead of seeing a smile, I noticed the anointing of the Holy Ghost on him; he pointed wildly at the pastor who was still sitting with his head leaning forward.

I spoke out aloud, asking Greg to explain the beer bottle. "Brother Yan," he said, I knew something was wrong here, but could not put my mind to it, until now. The Lord told me to walk up to that window," and he pointed at the window to the west. "When I walked up to the window, I noticed an empty bottle, and God said I must show it to you. That's when I placed it in front of you."

His voice was filled with emotion as he continued speaking. "Pastor, this man has a drinking problem."

"Are you saying, this empty bottle belongs to him?" I asked.

"No sir." The Lord directed me to the window, and that is when I saw the bottle. The bottle is not his, but it is only the evil symbol of what God wanted me to notice."

At first, I staggered at the accusation. The pastor lifted his head, and his eyes suddenly revealed guilt. He tried to deny it but stumbled over his words.

The Spirit of the Lord took charge of the moment, and then the pastor revealed and confessed his drinking problem.

There's more to this, Brother Yan. In fact, I don't believe one word this man is saying."

Suddenly, a can of worms opened up as we pressed in on the matter. We discovered that his wife was indeed a witch and the two of them had, in fact, defrauded our ministry with thousands of dollars over the past few years.

Looking back at that moment, I thank God for using men like Greg in my life. For some reason, I did not pick up on all of that, but God directed one of his servants to come to my aid.

"Now concerning spiritual brethren, I do not want you to be ignorant..."

These men and women who make themselves available to be used by the Lord, are a unique breed and worth having around as friends.

"DEMON POSESSED" LIONS

In my book, "You Won't Believe This," I share the story about two lions in front of a gate where we had to go through. These two young, male lions, were up to no good and when we tried to get them to move so that we could move forward. They attacked the car.

One of them tried to bite Bessie through the rear, side window, while the other sought to tear off the left front fender. He bit through the metal and left the evidence clearly on the paint of the brand new little Mazda which my sister loaned to me.

When I delivered the car back to her, I offered to have the car repaired, but she insisted on keeping it with the evidence clearly visible.

"How many lions do you know that attacked a car?" Annie asked.

Two years later, I was back in South Africa for another visit, but this time, Annie and Bertus, her husband, requested to go down to that same lion area with me.

When we arrived at my friend, Martiens' farm, I asked him to take Bertus and me to that same spot. "I want to go show him those lions," I smiled and said.

Although Annie and Bertus believed my story, Bertus himself being an adventurous person, insisted on taking a video of the incident.

Bessie decided not to film those crazy lions, and so Annie remained with her on the farm.

The Lion Park, made available their open Safari Jeep, so we set off to the same spot where the previous adventure took place.

I was very excited as we approached the area where those "demon possessed"[10] lions were.

Bertus insisted on standing at the back, behind the driver where he could handle the video camera better.

I was sitting with Martiens in the front when we came upon the lions. This time there were four of them! As we came to a standstill, they immediately approached the vehicle, sniffing on the tires and the bumper.

The rear window of the pickup had a slide in, which I kept open for communication with the camera man, Bertus.

As soon as the Lions started sniffing, I kept my eyes on the alert. That moment was extremely dangerous.

Those extremely dangerous and very agile animals surrounded the vehicle. They were not tame, and with one smooth movement, they could be on the back with Bertus in a heartbeat.

"Martiens, you have to be ready to move fast if something goes wrong," I suggested to that legend of the Lowveld.[11]

---

[10] I don't really believe they were demon possessed. I merely refer to them that way as I have NEVER heard of any lion attacking vehicles in that way. Especially since they were not provoked.

[11] Martiens Cronje who is now deceased, had become a legend in the Lowveld in his own right. His farm was nestled INSIDE the Kruger National Park. He was known by thousands of people, for hundreds of

Bertus had positioned himself in a wide stance, with his back against the cockpit of the vehicle as those dangerous animals were snooping around, on both sides of the jeep.

Of all the people I know, I only rate a few at my level of daring and Bertus rates very high on that list.

Talking to him through the little open window, I said, "Buddy, keep your eye on that guy by the bumper." Bertus slowly panned the camera towards the area of my concern. "That lion is up to something bad," I said, speaking more to myself.

His ears were pulled flat on his head, and the hair was standing up on his back.

With the camera rolling, Bertus spoke up and suggested to Martiens to slowly roll forward.

The next minute, that lion at the back, put both of his massive paws onto the rear bumper.

"Go Martiens, go. He's gonna jump onto the back of the jeep," I said without taking my eyes off the lion.

Martiens started to roll the vehicle forward, but another lion had moved into the path up front. We certainly did not want to harm any of these precious animals, but within moments, the situation had become dire at the back.

---

miles around because of his many adventures and interesting stories as a hunter, a guide, but also for his incredible love and knowledge about the wildlife and fauna and flora in that beautiful area of the Republic of South Africa.

"Faster Tiens," I suggested as the lion then managed to grab the tailgate of the Jeep, trying to get his rear legs onto the bumper.

I knew if he managed to do that, the next move would be to bite Bertus.

The moment became incredibly tense. Over my voice and also that of Bertus, crying out the importance of more speed, came the incredible roar of that menace in the back!

"Go, go, go," I instructed Tiens, who, up until that moment was trying to avoid the lion up front. With not a moment to spare, he accelerated as the lion at the back made his move.

He launched forward in an attempt to get to Bertus, but when he could not get his rear paws onto the bumper, he grabbed the rear seat of the Jeep and tore a large, gaping hole in it as he fell back onto the ground.

All of that time, that muscular, tall South African on the back, kept the camera rolling.

"Yahoo," he cried out in victory as we cleared the Lions.

We all laughed but realized at the same time how close to death, Bertus had come.

"Did you get all of that on video?" Tiens enquired.

"Yes sir, I did," Bertus proudly proclaimed. "We have the most incredible footage of Yan's 'demon possessed' lions in action!"

That night around the campfire, after a scrumptious South African dinner, everyone settled around the warm campfire and took turns to share our version of the story.

AN ELEPHANT IN THE CAR

Now and then, I will invite people, whom I think have the correct mindset for visits to Safari adventures in Africa.

That particular year, I arranged a mass crusade in Africa and several pastors were invited to accompany me. Among the invited ones, were a life-long friend of mine, Pastor Cleddie Keith.

Cleddie is well known throughout the USA and also many other parts of the world. The man has a natural love for God and also a desire to see people developed for the Kingdom of God.

Cleddie, like me, is a great storyteller with a rich inventory of good stories that can keep listeners spellbound for extended periods of time.

During one of my visits, I shared some of the Safari incidents with him and his friends. When the opportunity came for him to accompany me to Africa, I wanted to take this good friend of mine to the place where the lions attacked our vehicle.

I never did tell him of my intention, but I wanted to take him to the "demon possessed" lions.

In fact, I prayed and asked the Lord to make it possible for me to enlarge his inventory of stories.

When we arrived in that area where those lions were, it did not take me long to find them. My disappointment knew no limits though because they were laying down under the shadow of a huge Jackal berry tree. They did not show any interest in us, or in point of fact, in anything else for that matter.

Cleddie and his associate pastor took a variety of pictures, but there was no sign of any contrary movement by any of those killers of the jungle.

Finally, we slowly made our way back to our campsite.

That evening after everyone retired to bed, I walked around outside, praying.

I told the Lord how disappointed I felt and how much it would mean to those city slickers to go home with an interesting story to tell.

To me, it was not enough for my friends to merely "see" animals. "Lord, they need to EXPERIENCE" something. I smiled as I prayed with jest, saying to the Lord, "their visit with Yan Venter, has to contain adventure. Please Lord, give them something they will remember for the rest of their days."

As I finally laid down that night, I exhaled a long, deep breath. The lazy fan hanging from the ceiling had given up years ago against the never ceasing heat waves that can bombard those areas for months at a time.

That night was no exception. It seemed as if even the flies had no desire to continue their parade of irritation, as they were merely sitting in one position against the mosquito net hanging over my bed.

The familiar sound of night crickets filled the air. I listened very carefully to find any other sounds, but there were none.

After just a few minutes, I slipped into a deep sleep...

After an incredible Bush-Breakfast, we loaded the people into the safari vehicles to take them out on an excursion.

My friend, Martiens, was the guide.

The previous evening, I took him one side, explaining my disappointment.

"If at all possible, let's find something that can be above the norm for them to experience."

Martiens smiled and calmly said, "If it happens, then it will happen. We cannot MAKE it happen though. Let's see what the Lord has planned for us, ok."

He walked away but before he entered the vehicle in front of me, turned around and winked at me. I smiled, knowing that around Martiens, things always happen.

The morning drive produced nothing above normal. We finally stopped for lunch. Afterward, Martiens announced the importance for everyone to make a bathroom stop. "We will be in the vehicles for about four hours," he said.

For the following two hours, we scanned the bush for animals and good camera shots.

Everyone was hoping for a lion-kill or something of that sorts, but nothing of real excitement happened.

Cleddie was sitting next to me with his window rolled down, and his arm was resting on the door. His associate pastor, Vernell, seated alone on the back seat, hardly spoke as he enjoyed the slow movement through the African bush.

"Say, isn't that an elephant to our left?" Vernell broke the silence with a question.

I looked in the pointed direction and noticed a huge African Elephant bull, meandering our way.

The reader must understand that all the animals we run across, are wild. There is no "Zoo-Effect," with any of them. However, most of them are used to humans and cars.

I stopped the car and radioed to Martiens what we were seeing. They stopped their vehicle also and observed the same scene.

Just as the elephant came to about fifty feet from our car, I suddenly remembered my video camera was in the trunk of the car.

I left my door ajar as I quickly made my way to the trunk of the vehicle. Cleddie and Vernell turned to their left to observe that massive giant of the bush in its approach.

With the trunk filled with luggage, it took me a little longer to find my video camera. When I stepped back, armed and ready to shoot the approaching animal, I noticed to my delight; the elephant had positioned himself right against the little car we were traveling in.

He had two massive tusks which he laid on top of the roof of the car.

Toying with the car, he proceeded to bounce it up and down. With the camera rolling, I noticed the tires ballooning each time he pushed the vehicle down, and I was wondering how much those tires were going to handle.

The people in the first Safari vehicle were also filming the debacle.

Cleddie's window was still open, but he pulled his arm into the vehicle.

I heard him say to his associate, "Vernell, are you filming this?"

With a high pitched sound in his voice, he answered, "No!"

Cleddie wanted to know, why not.

"Because I'm scared," he admitted.

I was still on the outside, laughing and enjoying the moment when I noticed the massive trunk moving into the open door toward the unsuspecting Cleddie. He was apparently distracted by the closeness of that massive body, pressed real tight against the car and rocking it.

The trunk moved and searched in the process until he touched Cleddie's body from behind.

"Cleddie," I yelled. "look this way!"

Cleddie turned in my direction and then noticed the presence of the huge trunk, tickling him on his side.

I don't know who got the biggest scare, but the moment was very comical and certainly an adventure for them to remember, planned by God, in answer to my prayer, I'm sure.

One of the game wardens showed up and with great care, moved the friendly giant away from us.

He did admonish me, saying although the elephant meant us no harm, it could have had far-reaching effects if anything spooked the animal.

Although I understood what he said, nevertheless, I thanked God during my prayer time, because He allowed my friends to go back to the USA with a story to tell …

BLACK FRIDAY IN PRETORIA

People have no idea how much power their spoken words could carry. Even at times, when spoken in jest, it could easily create such a moment or experience.

When Cleddie's associate, Vernell, informed his wife of the opportunity with Yan Venter, she apparently protested gently, by saying to him, "I don't like for you to go with him, because you will come back, maimed, injured or cripple.

Driving back to Pretoria, following the visit to the Game Reserve, I felt right about the fact, that I had my friends with me in the car. I would not allow any harm to come to them.

We were nearing the end of our South African Safari and sitting behind the wheel, driving; I was pleased with all the events that occurred during their visit.

Cleddie was asleep in the back seat while Vernell was quietly looking around. We were all pretty much worn out, and Vernell spoke to me only when we had something to discuss.

A friend of mine made the little car available for us to use and I was very careful to keep it clean and to return it with no scratches to the vehicle.

The Elephant experience left two small marks on top of the roof where he rested his enormous tusks. The previous day, I spent hours rubbing and polishing the vehicle until those marks were hardly visible.

As we entered through a busy part of Pretoria, I was ready to return the car in a clean condition with a full tank of gas.

Although South Africa is not regarded as a Third World country and the traffic on its roads are well controlled by driving regulations, danger levels increase exponentially by taxi's driven by inexperienced or sometimes even unlicensed drivers. Most of the time they overload those vehicles with passengers.

The problem with "overload" runs through the veins of most drivers in the Third World. It does not matter if it's a bicycle, a motorcycle, a car or anything that has a wheel.

I have often seen up to six people on a small motorcycle and many times; I could not believe my eyes when they carried enormous amounts of stuff on a bicycle.

Most of the time, they pay little attention to traffic signs. Therefore, I knew the importance of looking or considering driving decisions twice before making them.

As we entered Pretoria, we were all happy that the long, arduous journey came to an end.

"Just a few more days," I said to myself, "and I could have my two friends at the Johannesburg airport, to return them safely to their families.

As we entered an intersection with the light indicating green for us, a "black taxi" appeared out of nowhere in front of us.

It had a woman driving the car, and she entered the intersection from my right at a great speed.

The impact was sudden and severe. In fact, I had no chance even to apply my breaks. The nose of our vehicle connected with hers in the middle, on the side, between the front and back doors.

The impact was so great, it turned our vehicle 180 in the air and then stopped where we "landed."

Later, the doctors told Cleddie, he was fortunate to be asleep, because the impact threw his body into the back of the driver's seat, escaping with only slight injuries.

Although Vernell had his seat belt on, somehow his head connected with the rear view mirror, cutting a deep slash across his forehead. At the same time, his left hip suffered enough damage, which he had to undergo surgery upon his return to the USA.

In fact, as they walked out at baggage claim, his wife was there to greet him. Vernell walked out, maimed, injured and crippled.

The injury scene was crazy. That medium size car had over a dozen bodies jammed into it, and following the impact, many of them catapulted like sandbags out of the car. No one wore a safety belt.

With consternation all around me and a large crowd of black people who surrounded the scene within minutes, I tried my best to remain sober.

Having grown up in South Africa, I realized the danger we faced. The black crowd increased quick, and I realized the danger we were in although it was not our fault.

Bodies were lying all around the scene, and I was relieved when the first of several other Ambulances showed up to be of assistance.

I've known my friend, Cleddie Keith, for more than thirty years. The man has a love for God like few men/women I know. In many circles, he's often referred to as "Mr. Revival."

From the moment he crawled out of our severely damaged vehicle, Cleddie walked up to me saying, "Brother, I feel the presence of the Holy Ghost around us."

Because of the pandemonium, I paid little attention to anything he was saying. I tried to find out who the driver of the other vehicle was, but someone told me she was dead.

Once again, Cleddie showed up behind me and whispered, "Yan, God is in this place," and then loudly broke out with speaking in tongues.

I felt sorry for Vernell who was sitting on the sidewalk with blood all over his shirt and a hip that was in severe pain.

Everywhere I turned, Cleddie was there to tell me about "the presence of God," until I felt a little irritated.

"I don't think he knows in what kind of danger we are finding ourselves in," I said to myself.

The first ambulance officer who showed up, walked over to me to confirm I was the driver of our vehicle.

Knowing that he and several others had attended to the injured of the other vehicle, I enquired about their situation.

"It's not okay," he answered with a concerned look, looking around him at the growing crowd. Many in the crowd were throwing angry looks my way.

"Are their injuries severe?" I asked but already knew about at least one dead body.

"Sir, the situation is dire. At least half of them are dead, and the injuries of some of the others are severe," he said as he glanced around again. I noticed his concern and I did not feel good.

The situation was ominous and looking at Vernell my fear grew even larger.

Suddenly, Cleddie was in my ear again from behind. He spoke a few words in tongues and then switched to English, saying, "Yan, the Master is here. I'm telling you this!"

Before I could respond to him, a young police officer walked over to me. We had already spoken as soon as he showed up to handle the scene.

This time, he walked up to me, taking me by the hand and pulled me aside. He said, "Mr. Venter, this situation is about to get out of control, you need to leave immediately. I have someone here who says they know you. They will drive you to your destination. Don't worry about the scene. I have your information and will be in touch with you soon. Right now, I need you and your passengers to leave immediately."

A few yards away from me, Cleddie was talking to God again, and I could tell he was in a world of his own.

I did not need much persuasion as I also felt the rising anger with a group of instigators standing in a huddle with sticks and other potential weapons in their hands.

I turned my attention back to the concerned officer and offered my protest; "Sir, I agree with your assessment, but what about the dead and injured?"

The officer motioned for the Ambulance man who briefed me about the situation, minutes ago to come to us. While the man made his way through the crowd towards us, the officer looked at me, saying, "There's no one dead. They're all okay."

"But..." I tried to tell him what the ambulance man informed me about, minutes ago, but then the Ambulance officer joined us.

The officer asked him to brief us about the scene once more.

The man had a confused look on his face when he looked at me, saying, "I just come from the other vehicle, and they're all okay. A few minor injuries. I honestly don't understand it, because there were several of them dead and I checked them myself."

He looked at the young officer and said, "Officer, I've never seen something like this. I'm not telling you a lie. I know there were people dead! The driver herself was dead, but when I checked on them again now, they're all alive. Every one of them!"

Suddenly, Cleddie showed up behind me again, smiling that time saying, "I told you, brother, God is in this place...!"

Only when I get to Heaven one day, will I be able to confirm the miracle, but believe me when I tell you this:

1. There were several dead.

2. There were serious injuries.

3. The report about all the above came from a seasoned ambulance man.

Since that accident, I have not taken Cleddie nor Vernell with me back to South Africa, but one thing I know and it is this:

GOD WAS INDEED AT WORK, THAT DAY!

THE 'INDIANA JONES' FIASCO.

A Gift in The Early Morning

Because of the numerous adventures, I've experienced in my life people from different walks of life, tried to label me as the Indiana Jones in the Assemblies of God, while others labeled me as Crocodile Dundee.

Nothing about my life has been normal. Therefore, any of the above labels could fit my life. Even my family members would agree.

However, the main reason I refuse to wear any of those badges is that I rather acknowledge the assistance of God in every situation instead of self-greatness.

I always tell people, "It never was Yan, it's always been God and God alone who saw me through these many experiences.

As I'm looking back, my life has been playing off like an adventure drama from Hollywood. The only difference was the fact that nothing was fake or merely the work of a stuntman. Every bit of all my experiences has been for real.

Some of my greatest stories played off while we were driving through this great nation with a forty-foot bus. Behind the bus, we always hauled one car or another.

During each and every journey, the tension was only a few seconds away, when we would have a blowout of a tire, or something going wrong with the engine. Anything about the engine would cost an arm and a leg.

The biggest thing I ever drove before coming to the USA, was a large 1974 Plymouth car. No one ever taught me about the do's or don'ts of bus driving. Every bit of our experience came through trial and error, which often made it dangerous.

In fact, whenever the bus moved, my passengers all became prayer warriors. Their ears always tuned to the slightest noise that should not be there. Never was there a car passing us by without us carefully observing the expressions of the motorists.

There were times when we had a puncture on one of the wheels of a trailer or car behind us, and the only way of knowing, would be when the driver pulled up next to us with arms wildly indicating the bad news.

Yes, we were all part of a traveling wonder, that was for sure.

This story starts in California where we had just lost a car on the bus as we slowly drove up and down Beverly Hills, admiring the homes of some of the Hollywood stars.

I told that story in a previous book, "You Won't Believe This."

Following the loss of that car, we continued to Simi Valley, to preach at one of the churches.

We arrived at the church's parking lot in the early evening, where we were allowed to connect our coach to their utilities.

That night we were utterly exhausted following the horrible experience of losing that car. I will never forget how close that ugly car came from colliding with a brand new, convertible Rolls Royce.

So, early evening, the Venter's were in bed, sleeping.

Around six the following morning there was a loud knock on the door of our Coach. It was something that never happened to us. People typically respected our privacy in the coach.

With uncombed hair and a sleepy expression on my face, I answered the door.

Two young ladies greeted me and asked, "Are you Brother Venter, the Evangelist?"

I confirmed and asked what I could do for them.

"Will you mind if we step into the Coach, Pastor?"

I really could not believe my ears. That had never happened to us anywhere. I explained that it was early and everyone was still sleeping.

The lead lady ignored my protest and said, "Pastor, we will not take your time long, but it is of the utmost importance that we take only a few minutes of your time.

Reluctantly, I stepped aside for them to enter and I seated myself uncomfortably opposite them. Both the ladies carried an air of excitement about them.

I paused to learn why they insisted on coming inside our small area of privacy.

When neither spoke up first, but merely stared at me with a weird kind of expectancy, I broke the silence by asking, "so, what can I do for you ladies?"

The smiling, leader, suggested I pray about "something."

"Ok, I will…" I said and waited for them to mention the prayer request.

"Brother Venter, the Lord will show you what to pray for," the tall, friendly one said.

I remember how frustrated it made me feel. I'm sitting opposite two strange ladies in a small environment; I have not even washed my face, nor brushed my teeth. I was woken up following a dreadful day, and now these ladies wanted to "play" that kind of game with me.

We bowed our heads in prayer, and I tried to wait on the Lord, but at that moment, I honestly felt no inspiration other than to see them leave so I could get into the shower.

After several minutes of "waiting," I scratched my head in a motion of frustration. Then the following words came out of my mouth after a long yawn: "Well ladies, I don't feel anything other than to say, that you should go ahead and do as the Lord already instructed you."

Suddenly, both of then jumped up from their seat in the coach and excitedly bounced up and down in front of me.

To be quite honest, it scared the living daylights out of me. I did not think I heard anything from the Lord and neither made any profound statement.

I sat speechless, until the tall one, grabbed her small purse, pulled a set of keys out of it and handed it to me. "Here's your car, brother Venter. The Lord told me to come over and give it to you."

This incident took place almost twenty years before the writing of this book, but I can clearly remember how stunned I was when she held the keys in front of me to take out of her hand.

"Now wait a minute," I said to her, "I cannot just take your car from you?" It was all I could say because I was totally overwhelmed. "How did this come about?"

As I was sitting there, I knew there was no way they or anyone else for that matter could have known about the car loss of the previous day. We came straight to the church in Simi Valley and after hooking up to the Church's utilities went to bed.

The tall one opened her purse again, pulled out a piece of scribbling paper and said, "Brother Venter, I am leaving for studies to Europe in a few days and was going to sell my car, when suddenly the Lord dealt with me to bring the car to you as a gift. My friend and I prayed and asked the Lord for confirmation. He told me to come to you, and you will say these exact words which I wrote down on that piece of paper. Please read it."

I took the piece of paper out of her hand, and it read, "You should go ahead and do as the Lord already instructed you."

Even though the evidence was there for me to read on that piece of paper, my head was still spinning for the moment.

She asked me to go outside to see the "little car."

There, parked neatly next to the bus, was an almost brand new, Ford Mustang!

It had but only a few thousand miles on the speedometer.

Once again, I tried to back away because of the severity of that gift.

My mind did not want to allow this to enter my world of reality. I thought that she was obviously still under the guardianship of parents, but after giving me a hug, she got into the friend's car and left me standing there, still mystified.

As soon as the pastor of the church showed up later that morning, I sat down in his office, explaining the events to him.

"Pastor, I brought the keys to you, and while I am incredibly humbled by this gift, I am hesitant to receive it," I expressed myself.

The pastor pushed the keys back to me and explained in a friendly way that they did seek his approval before going to our Bus, and that she also received her parents' permission. The loving man of God, leaned forward with his hands neatly folded in front of him.

"Brother Venter, her parents are extremely wealthy. They own several car dealerships amongst many other businesses, and you can rest assured, they can give you two of those cars and not even feel it."

Jumping for My life

The reason for losing our car in Beverly Hills, the previous week, was because the boom of the tow dolly broke.

Subsequently, when we left Simi Valley, Bessie was driving the car until we could get a chance to replace our tow dolly.

Our journey to the next church took us over the mountain pass at Paso Robles, on our way to Selma, California.

It was early afternoon as I passed a long uphill.

The Bus was doing well, although I knew to keep an eye on the heat gauge that was slowly climbing because of an unreasonably hot summer day.

Finally, I made the turn at the crest of the mountain pass, and immediately the heat gauge started to return to normal.

Bessie and our dog, Lady, were following behind me. Each time I made a sharp turn, my eyes would pick her up as she kept her safe distance.

Our minds were still reeling from the incredible experience when we that generous lady gave us that beautiful car.

It was a narrow, two-lane road, which demanded all my attention as I passed one sharp turn after another.

For a short distance, I crossed a straight section of the road, but then prepared for the upcoming next turn.

I can remember that the bus was moving at a speed of 55mph when calamity struck!

Following a loud popping sound, the steering in my hand leaned heavily to the left. I realized I suffered a blowout on the left front tire. The Bus was an older model and did not have power steering.

For a brief moment, I wrestled with the steering but noticed how dangerously close I had already come to the cliff to my left.

I was on a downhill trend and not able to slow the bus down as one should.

My speed was still around 50mph when I realized she was going over the side of the mountain and I had to make a decision in a short second.

I realized I was going to have to jump if I did not want to go with the bus down the dangerous cliff.

The next minute I let go of the heavy pulling steering and made a dash for the passenger door on the right side of the bus.

The entire event took place within a few seconds, but even as I write about it, I remember, it felt like an eternity before getting the door open and stepping out onto the road.

Before I stepped out, I already knew I was not going to be able to remain on my feet.

The moment I touched the road, the momentum threw me forward and down. I connected hard with the pavement and made sure I rolled away from the bus.

However, each time I turned, I noticed the approaching rear wheels. The momentum pulled me also toward the direction the bus was heading over the cliff.

On the last roll, the rear wheels were on top of me, but by then, the front left wheels went over the cliff, resulting in the right rear of the bus lifting enough to pass over me without touching me.

The next minute the bus went over the cliff and I followed behind…

As I rolled over the side, my hands caught a hold of a root of a tree, and I held on for dear life, as I watched our Coach roll and roll and roll.

A Highway Patrol Man, approaching from the opposite side, witnessed the entire event and also noticed my fall over the edge of the cliff.

Bessie saw the same and brought the car to stop on the shoulder of the road, next to the Patrol Car.

She was beside herself, as she rushed to the place where the bus went over.

The traffic officer grabbed my hysterical wife by the arm and tried to console her when suddenly I made myself heard a few feet down.

They helped me up, and the officer suggested I sit down somewhere while he radioed for Emergency Response.

I suffered severely lacerated wounds to both my arms and when the ER team arrived, they bandaged them, but the officer on the scene suggested I don't leave until they could recover the vehicle.

Several hours later, a huge crane was brought onto the scene to haul the remains of the Coach back up.

Only late that night I had the opportunity to show up at the hospital for treatment.

Looking back at the sequence of events, I know there would have been no way I would have jumped to safety if Bessie or anyone else for that matter, would have been on the bus.

Losing that ugly car, then the gift of the Mustang, all worked together for good as St. Paul explained to the Romans.[12]

---

[12] Matt. 8:28 "And we know that all things work together for good to them that love God, to them who are the called according to his purpose."

A DREAM ON FIRE

For several years, Bessie and I have been dreaming about building us a home here in the USA the way we wanted it.

Through the years we have been contemplating various ways in which we could accomplish that goal. Finally, we came upon the idea of purchasing a piece of property with a barn on it, and then to convert it into a dwelling.

Our plan was to live in the barn, debt free while we would slowly build our dream home little by little, on a cash basis.

After looking around for several years, we visited with friends of ours in Russellville, Arkansas.

Larry and Georgeanne Pyle have been very close friends of ours for more than a decade then, when they heard about our dream, Georgeanne said, "Yan and Bessie, I believe Larry and I have the ideal place for you!

This beautiful couple has been like family to us from the day we met them when Larry invited me to preach a Revival at their church in Russellville, Arkansas.

Larry, a man with a great sense of humor, yet quiet and reserved, is the total opposite from his lovely wife, Georgeanne. She is like a shot of adrenaline in anyone's life who interacts with her.

In her normal, happy way, Georgeanne clapped her hands excitedly in front of her as she jumped to her feet. "Come," she summoned all of us, "Let's go look at your new home."

We strolled down the three hundred yards from their house to the barn, while Larry explained the terms of sale. "We'll give you two acres of property if you will be willing to pay us what the barn cost us to erect."

He continued to tell us how it came about for them to purchase the barn.

Georgeanne and Bessie were walking in front of Larry and me. She bubbled over with joy at the thought of us becoming their neighbors.

Two months later, we unlocked our barn and stepped into it for the first time.

We were very excited. Bessie had her work clothes on, and as she stepped into the building, I could not help but admire her once again. She's a lady, through and through. I have never been embarrassed by her as my wife. She's a smart dresser and well-groomed by her mother, but she's never stepped back from work whenever I needed her help.

For the following three weeks, we worked as hard as I've ever worked, with Bessie and Eugene at my side. When we finally, opened the door for the carpet layers to do their job, we could not believe how well the project turned out.

We turned the ordinary pole-barn into a very efficient, four-bedroom home with two, full bathrooms. The house also included a large office for our ministry.

After moving our furniture into the house, and after Bessie completed her interior decorating, which she is superb at, the barn became a home, and we had every reason to be proud of it!

Over the next year, we worked as hard on the outside as Eugene, and I cleared the property from hundreds of trees, and the place became our dream come true.

The idea of building a home was no longer part of our thinking, and soon, I organized a workshop against the barn to accommodate my hobby as an accomplished woodworker.

In early January 2010, we had just woken up after a frigid night.

For several weeks, my two sons, CJ and Eugene, worked side by side with me on a furniture project for CJ and his wife. We finally had it complete and ready for the varnish after long days of sanding.

Inside the hobby shop, I had installed a wood burning stove, which I knew would come in handy during the cold winter months.

That morning, I instructed Eugene to start up a fire so we could get the finishing done. After several hours, I stepped outside into the adjoining shop to feel the temperature, but it was still freezing. Eugene's fire in the stove was dead and so I "encouraged" him to do a better job of the fire, and hurried back into the house where it was warm.

The frustrated Eugene, went next door where one of our neighbors were building a house. Eugene gathered scraps of pine wood and stoked the stove with a full load of the hot burning wood.

In ignorance, he left the loading door slightly ajar as he hurried into the warm house, causing the fire to spill out onto the rubber mats on the floor and setting it on fire.

CJ and I were sipping on our second cup of coffee while we talked about our plans for the day.

Bessie was still in bed, not feeling well that day. Her Mother is an early riser and that morning was no exception. However, because of the cold, she kept to her room.

The construction workers next door said they saw smoke rise from the house and then rushed over to our house to investigate.

Inside the house, I looked up to the crown molding on the opposite side of the room where smoke started billowing forth.

It took all of us a few seconds to realize the danger, but then CJ cried out, "There's a fire, dad!" All of us made a dash for the outside door, and as we stepped outside, we met the construction workers outside ready also to investigate the fire.

I opened the shop door and as I did, the fresh oxygen flowing into the room, caused an explosion of the thick sanding dust in the shop combusted.

The flames in the little hobby shop quickly spread. One of the men reached for the hose pipe outside the shop, but because of the cold condition, we found the hose pipe frozen solid.

CJ ran inside, yelling at the three ladies to come outside.

I will never forget the panic on my wife's face as she ran outside with her little dog safely in her arms. Flames were now recklessly devouring the inside. Suddenly, Bessie remembered that her purse was inside with the only money we had in it, and before anyone could stop her, she rushed madly into her bedroom, with CJ following behind. The house filled with an ugly gray smoke very quick.

Pandemonium broke out and as the two of them reappeared. It was then that we noticed the carport were catching fire. The bumpers of the two cars inside were already starting to burn. Bessie threw her purse on the floor as she rushed into one of the vehicles, with Anelda, our daughter in law, getting behind the wheel of the second car.

The keys of that vehicle were in the house, so the men pushed it into safety by hand.

When Bessie stepped back into the carport to retrieve her purse, the flames already consumed it. Only then did she realize she only had one slipper on and the other foot bare. Sobbing with total frustration, she pulled the lonely slipper from her foot and threw it into the fire also.

Our neighbor, Larry Pyle, rushed to our side, telling us he already called the Fire Department, but because it is staffed by volunteers, it took almost an hour before they showed up.

Out of all the stories in my life, that day will stand out all on its own as the most devastating moments in all my life. Standing there and helplessly watching the flames do its horrible work, burning through a lifetime of sermon collections and all sorts of ministry materials will never be forgotten as long as I live.

Bessie's beloved grand piano, many oil paintings from several famous painters, family photo albums and much more, were being consumed by an "enemy" that seemed to follow its agenda.

By the time the Fire Department showed up, not much could be done, other than to put the flames out. Those precious men, whom we will always be thankful for, fought those flames valiantly, but finally, when only the lingering smoke remained, what the flames did not get, the water destroyed the rest!

Friends and neighbors came and surrounded us with love and affection. Larry and Georgeanne lovingly put their arms around us and offered up loving prayers of compassion. I will never forget his words, as him and Georgeanne wept with us; he said, "God, today the enemy dealt the Venter's a severe blow, but I am accusing the opponent in this one. Whatever he took from this family, we ask in Jesus Name, for him to pay back double..."

Before the day was through, we had several thousand dollars that people brought to us with love and great affection.

We were devastated as we finally were allowed to search through the fire rubble to save the little we could. A beautiful dream went up in smoke and flames in one cold, dreary morning.

I cannot end this story without giving full credit to State Farm Insurance company, for the way they stood with us throughout that ordeal.

Three days later, Bessie and I started making plans to rebuild. We realized it would not be wise to spend money on fixing the barn, so we began to look into the possibility of building a new home.

After praying about the matter, the Lord directed me to contact a dear friend, Bob Lowery, in Myrtle Beach, South Carolina, who is a very successful Architect and his wife, a well sought after, interior decorator.

They had no knowledge about our tragedy, but when he answered the call, he said, "Brother Venter, what a pleasant surprise to hear from you!" He talked for a while and then said, "I am amazed that you would call me today?" When I asked him why that was, he informed me that he had a dream about us the night before.

"What was the dream about, Bob?" I still did not have a chance to say anything about the devastation of the past few days. Bob laughed in his usual delightful manner, saying, "Brother, I designed you the most beautiful home…"

For a moment I was stunned, but then I told him what had happened. Bob smiled on the other side when he said, "Well Brother Venter, I believe God is in this thing. Why don't you get on an airplane and fly to South Carolina? I will have the plan on paper when you get here.

CJ and I came back from Myrtle Beach only a few days later, with plans for the most beautiful home we have ever seen. It was more than twice the size of our burned out home, with everything we've ever dreamed about.

When I complained to Bob that the house was too big, he smiled and said, "Brother, you'll have to talk to God about it. He gave me the plan, and I am not changing it. The rest is between you and Him."

After the builders had laid out the foundation to the home, he called us to have a look. With genuine concern in his voice, the kind Contractor said, "Brother Venter, this house is humongous! I thought you should see with the footings in place. If you want to downsize this house, now will be time to do it. It's going to be very expensive!

I smiled at the kind man but told him that God designed the house for us, and we're not changing it.

Later, after the floor was in, he called us in again, to come, "walk the house," as he put it. The place was huge. Almost five and a half thousand square feet.

For a moment, I hesitated when he insisted on cutting the house down in size again. Our son, CJ, stood next to me and spoke up on my behalf. "Sir, we appreciate your concern, and we understand what you are saying, but you must understand we had nothing to do with the design of this house. God designed it for my parents. We are not cutting down on the size of the house. You build it, and God will provide the finances…"

In less than six months later, the Venters moved into a dream house which God made possible.

The day we dedicated the house, we remembered the words of Larry Pyle when he asked God to make the enemy give back twice what he has stolen.

The house is exactly twice the size of the one that burned!

A PIANO GIFT

One of the great losses in the fire was Bessie's Baby Grand piano.

Watching the fire and then the subsequent water does its damage was one of the hardest things we've had to endure.

"Bessie, God, is at work in this thing and I am convinced that the matter of your piano will also be resolved," I told her.

We invited several of our closest friends for the house dedication. Pastor Brad and Cathy Westover from Johnstown, Pennsylvania, drove 1,110 miles to honor us on that beautiful day.

To our surprise, Brad informed us they brought a housewarming gift and asked us to step outside to their vehicle where they had the most beautiful Baby Grand piano in the back of a trailer.

The reason I want to add this information to my book is that of the incredible way the entire thing played off.

The story started twenty years before our fire damage. Brad was on his way to purchase a boat when suddenly the Lord instructed him to stop at a music store first.

The moment he saw the piano, the Lord told him to buy it even though no one in his home played that instrument, but he obeyed the voice of the Lord nevertheless.

To the amazement of Cathy, his wife, they delivered the piano to her home where it remained under a soft cover and hardly ever played.

Cathy, one of the most beautiful people we know, with a pleasant, sweet personality, did not understand Brad's decision but settled on the idea that if the Lord told him to do something, she would not stand in his way.

A few days before their departure to come to us, the Lord woke him up early one morning and told him to load the piano as a gift to "Yan and Bessie."

Just think about the enormity of the story! Twenty years before the fire, God already provided a replacement for our loss!

He picked out the same color as the one damaged in the fire and kept it in a safe place until the time of delivery…

Ecclesiastes 3:14-15, "I know everything God does endure for all time. Nothing can be added to it; nothing can be taken away from it. We humans can only stand in awe of all God has done. What has been and what is to be—already is. And God holds accountable all the pursuits of humanity." [*Voice Translation.*]

ANOTHER AIRPLANE SAGA

Where's the wheels?

For several long weeks, I have been waiting on my Aircraft Mechanic to notify me of the completion of the regular annual service.

Working on the new church in Waco, TX turned out more than a normal challenge for me. Russellville, AR, (Where we live) is five and a half hours away if there's no traffic hold-up, whereas, with my airplane, I did it in less than an hour. So, needless to say, I was very anxious to get back in the air.

I knew better than to rush the mechanic because I needed to be sure the aircraft was definitely airworthy. (Airworthiness is the measure of an aircraft's suitability for safe flight. Certification of airworthiness is initially conferred by a certificate of airworthiness from a national aviation authority, and is maintained by performing the required maintenance actions by an approved FAA qualified aircraft mechanic.)

I also knew there was no way that my mechanic would tolerate any unnecessary phone calls.

Finally, after a few more weeks, the long expected call came and it could not have happened at a better time for me. Bessie and her Mom, Miemie, were visiting me in Waco and needed to return home.

"Mr. Venter, your plane is ready, and she is fully functional", the mechanic said.

Early the following morning I was waiting outside his shop, and as soon as he arrived, he took me to the airplane to do the usual walk around it, explaining his work. Finally, he signed the aircraft back to me, but added the following; "Mr. Venter, she's doing great. Everything has been checked out, but when we checked the landing gear, everything worked smooth, except for the Emergency Crank handle behind the front passenger seat. For some reason, it is real tight. I know you need to take your family back to Arkansas, but when you come back next week, bring the plane to me so I can check out what is causing the problem. If you ever need to use that crank, you are going to have a problem because of your arms. Since I fell off the four-story building, my left arm has no elbow, and the right arm is also in poor a condition and not able to handle much stress.

I've flown for many years, but I've never had a need to use the emergency crank. It is a small little handle of about six inches long and is situated uncomfortably behind the front passenger seat near the floor. It is designed to function smoothly, and the pilot can operate it by reaching down and back to the bottom, next to him while he flies the plane.

After assuring him I would comply with the request, we proceeded to fuel the aircraft. The fuel at St. Marcos, Texas, was almost a dollar per gallon higher than Waco, TX, and for a brief moment, I contemplated to fill just enough to reach my destination, with an hour extra as required by regulation. While the Mechanic fueled my plane, I suddenly felt an urge to fill all the tanks, and I asked him to do so. "Just in case," I said smilingly, not knowing how important this decision would prove to be.

I felt good when the familiar feeling of satisfaction came over me, as the Baron lifted her wheels up from the runway, and within a few short minutes, I reached my altitude of five thousand feet. She was flying well, according to my calculation, I would reach Waco in twenty minutes.

At takeoff, I carefully observed the operation of the landing gear, but they worked as they should, and I heard the little pop when the wheels pulled up under the belly of the airplane. I could not help but smile when I noticed how I stressed after flipping the gear-up button and then the relief when it completed its cycle.

The short flight was a pleasure and a little quicker than usual because of a relatively strong tailwind. The tower at the Waco airport gave me approval for my approach and cleared me to land on runway one.

As soon as I reached the required Pattern Altitude, I reached forward and flipped the gear-down button and waited with anticipation for the gear to come down. My eyes remained fixed on the "lock-down" indicating light that should come on, but then nothing happened. To the left of me, on the side of the engine, a small mirror allows the pilot to see the gear, but nothing was visible.

The gear did not come down!

I announced my intention to circle the airport as I recycled the gear by flipping the switch again and again. But nothing happened!

As required by regulation, I announced to the tower what the status was and the controller suggested I do a low fly-by the tower so that they can take a look at the plane to see if anything was wrong.

Bessie and her Mom was sitting in the car close to the landing strip, waiting for my arrival, but when she noticed the circling of the airport with no wheels down, she said to her mother, "something is wrong. Yan's landing gear is not down!"

Stress levels soared high on the ground as well as in my cockpit. The very thing the mechanic said would cause trouble was playing off.

It was an incredibly hot day, and suddenly it dawned on me, I had no water.

As I flew passed the tower as slow as possible, I lifted my left wing to offer a better opportunity for then to take a look. The controller came on the air and said, "N2709T, your doors did not even open. There's no sign of any obvious problems. What is your intention?"

The adrenaline pumped fast into my system, but I took a long, deep breath before replying. "Waco Tower, I'm going to climb back up to five thousand and then make an attempt to bring the gear down manually."

The tower gave me a course to fly and assured me they would clear all traffic away from me.

As soon as I reached my altitude, I checked and found the Tripped Circuit Breaker. It tripped again after each reset. Realizing there's a problem, I made sure the breaker remained pulled out. (You don't want to have your hand on the crank handle and suddenly the gear starts to operate again. It can easily break your hand.")

Reluctantly, I reached for the handle, but as I tried with all my strength to turn it, I managed only a half a turn with a great effort. I sat back and took a deep breath. "Think, Yan. Think."

I realized I had only two options. Although the manufacturer designed the aircraft for a belly landing, I did not wish to choose that option as I did not want to lose my plane, so I decided on the second alternative.

The only way I could properly attempt to get the crank handle to turn would be to rely on the autopilot to fly the airplane as I situated myself on the floor behind the pilot seat. I announced to the tower that I was going to be "off air" while attempting this operation. The autopilot handled the plane on a straight and level flight as I climbed over the seat to the back and positioned myself, facing the handle.

As I climbed over the seat to the back, I said to myself, "this must be one of the dumbest things you've ever attempted in your life."

My adrenaline was now pumping at its highest level. The operation was extremely dangerous, and if any pilot is reading this story, you will possibly judge it as incredibly reckless. However, I did not want to lose my plane, and I had confidence in the autopilot.

My struggle with the crank handle started. It took all my effort to turn it once, and I knew I had to complete at least 50 revolutions or more.

It was one of the hottest days in Texas and with all the struggle to get the gear down, I developed one of the worst thirsts I ever experienced, but I had no water with me. My tongue stuck to the top of my mouth as I struggled with this task.

I was in an awkward position with my one leg bent beneath me and leant on one knee, when suddenly the autopilot threw me into a steep bank to the left and a dive.

The moment caught me in a surprise, and that action caused me to stumble sideways with my back against the pilot seat.

I realized I did not have much time to recover as I was in a suicide dive. Pandemonium struck as I was half stuck in between the seats. I reached my arms backwards and grabbed the yoke, trying to pull it out of the dive and to bring it back to level flight. The autopilot was still engaged and did not allow me to control the airplane. My fingers found the disconnect button on the yoke, but as I pushed it, the autopilot would not disengage. I pushed myself, still backwards, onto the seat and it folded forward, allowing me to reach the autopilot control on the console.

One day when I reach heaven, I'm sure someone will inform me of the presence of an angel that day. I found the "on/off" switch in a rearward position and the autopilot disengaged, allowing me to pull the yoke back and bring the airplane level.

My one leg was stuck in an uncomfortable position, and with extreme pain, I pulled and freed myself, allowing me to turn around and bring everything back under control.

I was flying the airplane from the back seat, bringing her back to five thousand feet. Sweat was pouring down my face and into my eyes. My body temperature was higher than ever in my life, and my tongue was stuck to the top of my mouth.

"Baron N2709T, what just happened?" The urgent request came from the controller, but when I responded, my speech came out almost unrecognized. I took a deep breath, and tried a second time, talking real slow, assuring them I was ok, but struggling to get the gear down.

For the second time, I carefully set the autopilot and continued the quest to master the task ahead of me, this time, making sure I positioned myself in such a way that I would not repeat the same situation.

Twice more, the autopilot did the same thing, but each time, I was prepared for it and handled the situation better.

After each five minute intervals, I had to reach forward to adjust my course so that I did not fly too far away from the Waco airport.

The struggle went on for almost three hours. I had no idea how many revolutions I completed, so I struggled to slowly turn the crank until finally, it did not want to crank anymore.

The lock-down indicator was not lit up, which would mean that it was not safe to land the airplane. If the gear is not locked down, upon landing, it could fold up and quickly flip the airplane. I knew it, but for the first time in my entire life, I reached a point of total exhaustion. There was not a grain of strength left in me. My body needed water. I was close to heat exhaustion.

With great effort, I pushed the talk button and informed the worried controller of the situation.

The Tower replied, "N2709T, I have a mechanic with me, and he says if the lock-down signal light is not on, it will not be safe to land the airplane."

I replied, "Waco, I have tried everything possible. The crank will not turn anymore; I am totally spent and almost out of fuel. I am bringing the airplane in for a landing."

There was a short silence before the response came. "N2709T, you are cleared to land on runway one. Good luck."

As I approached, I looked at my cell phone and noticed I had full reception. Bessie was waiting on me, and I had enough time to text her.

"Honey, I'm coming in, to land, but things don't look good. Pray for me."

She responded, "You're going to be okay, Baby. I have been praying." I recognized the stress in her tone, and I knew she was fighting the emotions of the moment.

For a few moments, I pondered my next text as I realized it could be my last.

I texted, "Baby, we've had a good run together for 47 years. Remember, we have no regrets," then there was no more time for the phone because I had arrived on the threshold of the runway. I threw the phone one side, put my hands on the yoke, and allowed my eyes to check my airspeed. I came in barely above stall speed. "This will have to be a soft landing," I said to myself.

On the ground, Bessie stood next to the runway as I flew slowly past her. She could see me in the cockpit. Her Mom was anxiously watching the drama from inside the car.

Bessie threw her cell phone on the ground, pointing her finger at the airplane and with a voice filled with a supernatural faith, shouted the words out; "You will land safely, in the Name of Jesus!"

In the cockpit, I was calm. Peace came over me as I did what I was trained to do. Very gingerly, I allowed the airplane to a touchdown and then I lifted her up again slightly.

Before I set her down again, the voice of the controller came on the air, this time without my call sign, but I could hear the angst in his voice; "The gear looked solid, sir."

I could not help but force a tired smile to my face, and then I let the airplane softly sit down...

The local mechanic came out to the airplane to check out the situation. After checking the landing gear, he looked up at me and said, "Mr. Venter, this gear should not have held you up. The lockdown interlock did not engage. Someone was looking out for you."

Bessie's Account

"Honey, please meet me at the Waco airport, in about one hour from now" Yan's call reached me around 9 am in the morning.

My mother and I started out toward the airport and made a quick stop on our way. We arrived at the Waco airport about 15 minutes before Yan's scheduled arrival.

To watch his landing, we positioned ourselves close to the beginning of the runway. For some reason, I struggled with an eerie feeling as I waited.

"Something is not right," I said to myself but kept my feelings hidden from my Mom.

Finally, I heard the sound of the engines, but as I watched the approach of our airplane on final approach, he suddenly pulled back up and flew past me without landing.

Immediately I noticed the landing gear was not out and then the feeling of unrest all morning long, made sense. "Mom, something is not right. The landing gear is not out," I uttered my concern, as the airplane engines made a louder noise when Yan climbed back to the pattern altitude and circled the airport.

I knew Yan were manually attempting at correcting the problem.

I leaned over to my mother and suggested to start praying. Baffled, she wanted to know what was going on but all I could do was to cry out; "the landing gear did not come down, Mommy."

"Oh boy," I spoke again. "Calling on God is our only answer, Mom."

We held hands, and my loving mother and I started to call on God for help with that situation.

We watched as Yan flew very slowly past the control tower, lifting up his one wing as he passed, but then turned into a southerly direction and disappeared.

I was stunned and confused at the same time. "Why did Yan fly away from the airport, and where is he going? Why was the gear not down? Dozens of questions went through my head, causing me to feel dizzy.

After about a half an hour with no sign of the aircraft, I called the airport, and the kind manager filled me in about the problem, after telling him I was Yan's spouse. He confirmed my suspicions. He explained that Yan was trying to get the gear down manually.

I was going out of my mind with concern when he stayed away for more than two hours.

Finally, I stepped out of the car, and walked up to the fence close to the beginning of the runway, and started praying in tongues very loudly. My Heavenly Father now was the only one who could control this situation.

After what seemed an eternity, I finally heard the approaching airplane, and then I received a text from my Yan, saying we needed to pray....

I replied back telling him we were acutely aware of the situation and we were praying and believing for God to assist him in that situation.

With a firm, calm voice I texted, "Honey, you are going to make it!"

As the airplane slowly approached the runway where I was standing, I prayed louder and louder.

"SATAN, IN THE NAME OF JESUS, I COMMAND YOU TO TAKE YOUR HANDS OFF THAT AIRPLANE, AND BY THE POWER OF THE HOLY SPIRIT, LANDING GEAR... WE INSTRUCT YOU NOT JUST TO COME DOWN, BUT TO STAY DOWN FOR THE LANDING."

At first, I thought the plane was not moving at all, just hanging still in the sky, but then I realized he was coming in extremely slow.

My phone indicated another incoming text. It was Yan again, saying, "Honey, we've had a great run together for forty-seven years, and we have no regrets…"

My legs wanted to fold in under me as I read the text, but then I experienced a tremendous surge of God's power running through my body.

As the airplane approached the threshold, I threw my phone down away from me, as if it was the problem. I lifted my hand, stretching it out toward the airplane, and commanded the landing gear to stay down and support the aircraft.

I watched as Yan put the airplane down softly and the landing gear stayed down. PRAISE THE LORD!!!!

With a feeling of renewed awareness of life, I jumped into the car and rushed to the other side of the airport where I knew Yan would park the plane.

As soon as the airplane came to a stop at the parking area, I saw the airport staff surrounding him to offer praises for being so courageous. Even the Air Controller was out there to offer congratulations.

Looking at Yan, I realized I've never seen my husband like that. Sweat dripped from him like streams of water. Yan was smiling, but I could see he was exhausted.

"Thank you, Jesus!"

It was not the first time God gave him back to me. No matter how hard the devil tried to kill Yan before and there were many other instances.

I realized that God still had much for Yan to do in the Kingdom of our Savior!

The Lord still needed him. Without an airplane, without a left elbow and even after bringing him back from the dead when he fell off a four-story building, this valiant husband of mine, still stands stronger than ever before.

In spite of all the attacks of the enemy, he still carries out the work of our Father with as much zeal as before.

As I waited my turn to get to Yan, with the group of airport staff members crowding him, I realized that this incident was just another valley to go through or another mountain to climb.

I'm anxiously waiting to see how this will finally turn out because God says in His word, "And we know that all things work together for good to them that love God, to them who are called according to his purpose. Rom. 8:28

I give God all the glory!

YOU MUST BE KIDDING...

Following the problem with the landing gear, the FAA grounded the airplane until the problem have been taken care of by a reputable aircraft mechanic. So, the wait started once again, and I was more than frustrated.

The report from the mechanic came in, informing me that the gearbox of the landing gear needed to be replaced. The estimated cost was going to be around eight thousand dollars.

I needed the airplane, so, I gave them the green light to continue.

The aviation company regularly worked on Beechcraft Baron airplanes, and I rested assured that they were competent to carry out the required repairs.

After almost two months, the call came in that the airplane was ready.

When I inspected the airplane with the manager of the company at the handover, the man assured me that it was like brand new. He said, "Mr. Venter, we put the airplane on jacks and had the gear go up and down seven times. It works just fine, and you can fly her this time with no concern."

I needed to fly home, so I had them top off all the fuel tanks and the following morning, I departed early.

When I received the weather report, it indicated cloudy conditions over the first leg, but then clear conditions.

The Weather condition required IFR rules.

Instrument flight rules (IFR) indicate and dictate how aircraft are to be operated when the pilot is unable to navigate using visual references under Visual Flight Rules. For the aircraft to be flown in instrument meteorological conditions (IMC), it must be fitted with the necessary instrumentation and certified by the regulatory authority. In addition to this, the pilot must hold an instrument rating.

Before a pilot flies under IFR rules, he is required to submit an IFR flight plan to the air traffic control. Such a flight plan allows for aircraft separation in controlled airspace, and for traffic information to be provided to aircraft operating in uncontrolled airspace for the pilot to be separated from other traffic sufficiently.

The IFR Pilot is further required to stick to the flight plan at all time and remain in constant radio contact with air control.

The takeoff was smooth, and while I ascended to the filed altitude, my eyes scanned the instruments carefully as I entered the clouds. For several minutes I flew blind but then suddenly, I broke through the clouds and experienced the excitement of being above the white bed beneath. The morning air was clear and with a relatively strong tailwind from behind, the Baron moved forward at above average cruising speed.

I kept myself occupied by studying various landmarks and comparing it with my aviation maps while the autopilot did most of the work for me.

In my headset, soft music helped to relax me even further. I was going to make real time and finally laid the maps down, allowing my eyes to scan the vast open horizon.

A few cumulonimbus clouds were hanging triumphantly at different positions in front of me, and I allowed the Baron to graciously fly around them. I was enjoying the flight.

At around the halfway mark, suddenly, things went wrong.

I noticed all the lights of my autopilot were flickering which is not normal. I allowed my eyes to glance over the rest of the instruments and noticed the lights of my GPS were off.

I reached for the radio push-to-talk button and called the air controller but found the radio also cut off. This was not good.

In IFR conditions, if I suddenly disappear, Air Control have no way of knowing what happened, and it could spark all sorts of search and find procedures from their part. So, I knew, this was not good at all.

I pulled out my Aircraft manual and checked on possible causes for the autopilot to blink the way it did. After another fifteen minutes, I found my answer, so I followed the recommended procedures by recycling the first alternator. Immediately the power came back on, so I proceeded with the second alternator, and it came on also.

I sighed a relief when I noticed my radios were back online and immediately called on Air Control to report.

"N2709T, you had us very concerned. What happened?"

For the next few minutes, I briefed them on my situation and assured them if it happened again, I would land at the nearest airport and contact them by telephone.

I was sitting up straight, and my back strained with contracting muscles because of the stressful situation.

Several times, the same thing happened again, but each time, I was responding on time, ensuring continued radio contact.

My eyes glanced over all my instruments and scanned around inside the aircraft for any sign of smoke. I realized that I was dealing with an electrical problem, but I pushed on to get home as soon as possible.

Several times, Air Control would contact me to find out if I was still doing fine.

Slowly the clouds beneath me started to clear, and I was relieved to see the ground. "The last thing I need today is to have to make an emergency landing, without being able to see the ground," I mumbled to myself.

A few minutes later, I saw the mountain range around Russellville, and I received clearance from air control to start a slow descent.

Disgust rose in my spirit because of the continued problems with the airplane but decided to put it out of mind until I could get her on the ground.

Suddenly, the power went out again, but that time the recycling of the alternators only lasted for a short while before losing cutting out again.

I contacted Air Control, saying, "Memphis, this is N2709T."

"This is Memphis, N2709T, what can we do for you?"

"Memphis, I'm experiencing ongoing problems, and I have the airport in sight. I would like to cancel my flight plan as I'm in VFR conditions. Request permission to change frequency to the local airport at Russellville."

"N2709T, your flight plan is cancelled. Contact Russellville. Have a good day."

With the airport in sight at pattern altitude, I contacted Russellville, announcing my approach.

"N2709T, runway seven is in use, and the wind is calm."

I flipped the gear-down switch and waited to hear the sound of the driving gear, but then nothing happened! I suddenly felt sick in my stomach. I could not believe what was going on. I worked the switch again, keeping my ear tuned and my eye on the small mirror on the side of the left engine, but nothing was happening.

"I don't believe this," I said out loud. "Not again?"

I checked for the CB, and sure enough, it was in the tripped position. Several attempts to get it to stay on failed and with utter disgust, I reached for the crank handle to my right near the floor behind the front passenger seat.

This time, there was not even the slightest movement. It was stuck tight.

"Russellville, this is N2709T, I'm having problems with my landing gear. I'm going to circle the runway."

The manager came on the air as he recognized my voice, "Yan, there is no traffic in the area. Take your time; we will get the fire department here just in case you will need it.

Your wife is here, and she heard what is going on. I'm sorry, but she looks okay."

I started to circle the airport and decided to circle until I could burn off most of the fuel in my tanks.

Suddenly, the power went offline again, but this time I could not get it back on.

My heart flipped when all of a sudden, smoke started to appear from under the dashboard.

"This is not good," I said to myself. I reached for my fire distinguisher by my feet and laid it on the seat next to me. All of a sudden more smoke appeared and then I realized my problem is more than what I wanted to handle.

I had no radio to contact the airport, but when I looked down to my left as I flew the pattern upwind, I noticed the fire trucks pulling into the airport. Bessie stood next to her car; then I brought my eyes back to the airplane, inside.

"Fly the plane, Yan. Be calm," I instructed myself.

The smoke became thicker as I turned on final approach, and decided not to use the fire distinguisher.

"I'm going to put her down on her belly this time," I said to myself.

A calm took hold of my mind, and I said a prayer as I readied myself for the emergency landing. I made one last check to make sure I am doing things according to the provided checklist. The runway was in front of me, and I was coming in low with a slow approach.

With all the fuel still unused, I was not going to take a chance to get caught inside the cockpit, so I opened the passenger door before I touched down.

Ever so gently, I brought her down, and for a while, it seemed as if she was just hovering above the landing strip, but then the belly touched the ground.

The grinding noise was loud, and smoke was visible inside and out.

As soon as the airplane started to slide on the pavement, I waited no longer. I made my way to the door and stepped out onto the right wing while the airplane was still sliding.

As soon as it came to a halt, I jumped off the wing and noticed the fire truck behind me.

"Goodness, sir, how did you get out of the airplane that fast?", The Fireman asked. I only smiled at him in reply.

The next minute the fire department took control and doused the airplane with water inside and out.

Unfortunately, instead of using the correct foam to put the fire out inside the cockpit, the water destroyed almost fifty thousand dollars' worth of instruments inside the plane.

The aircraft remained on the runway until the FAA could carry out an inspection.

Their final report stated:

"Mr. Venter demonstrated airmanship of the highest quality."

They also found that the limit switch which allowed the retraction of the gear to stop at a certain point did not function as it should which resulted in the gear pulling up too far, resulting in it getting jammed.

They struggled for more than an hour to get the gear unstuck and finally used a pry bar to get it to release.

At the time of this writing, the FAA had not yet released their finding on the work of the Aviation Company.

The Insurance Company totaled the plane, but because we tried to keep the insurance payments to a minimum, we suffered an enormous financial loss.

One thing is for sure though. I take no credit for airmanship. All credit goes to the Lord, and I will forever be thankful to the Lord for His protection.

As soon as I reached Bessie and her Mom after the landing, she put her arms around me and said, "Honey, this is enough. I cannot handle any more of this. Please get rid of that airplane."

Her tone assured me she was not asking, but she insisted most certainly.

Although that was the end of the Beechcraft Bonanza, I am still praying and believing the Lord for another airplane…

Made in the USA
San Bernardino, CA
16 July 2017